Guide to

Managerial Communication

Effective Business Writing and Speaking

Guide to

Managerial Communication

Effective Business Writing and Speaking

Seventh Edition

by Mary Munter
Tuck School of Business
Dartmouth College

PRENTICE HALL
Upper Saddle River, New Jersey 07458

For Paolo, Giulia, and Lorena

Library of Congress Cataloging-in-Publication Data

Munter, Mary.
Guide to managerial communication : effective business writing and speaking / by Mary Munter.—7th ed.
p. cm.
Includes bibliographical references and index.
ISBN 0-13-146704-2 (alk. paper)
1. Business communication. 2. Communication in management. 3. Writing (in business). 4. Presentations (in business). I. Title.
HF5718.M86 2005
658.4'5—dc22

2005042190

Acquisitions Editor: Ashley Santora
VP/Editorial Director: Jeff Shelstad
Associate Director of Production: Judy Leale
Production Editor: Marcela Boos
Permissions Coordinator: Charles Morris
Associate Director, Manufacturing: Vincent Scelta
Production Manager: Arnold Vila
Manufacturing Buyer: Michelle Klein
Cover Design: Kiwi Design
Manager, Print Production: Christy Mahon
Composition: BookMasters, Inc.
Full-Service Project Management: Jennifer Welsch, BookMasters, Inc.
Printer/Binder: R.R. Donnelley–Harrisonburg
Typeface: Times

Pearson Education LTD.
Pearson Education Australia PTY, Limited
Pearson Education Singapore, Pte. Ltd
Pearson Education North Asia Ltd
Pearson Education, Canada, Ltd
Pearson Educaciōn de Mexico, S.A. de C.V.
Pearson Education–Japan
Pearson Education Malaysia, Pte. Ltd

10 9 8 7 6 5 4 3 2 1
ISBN 0-13-146704-2

Contents

INTRODUCTION v

I

COMMUNICATION STRATEGY 2

Communicator Strategy 4
Audience Strategy 10
Message Strategy 18
Channel Choice Strategy 23
Culture Strategy 29
Strategy Checklist 32
Guide to the Guide 33

II

WRITING: COMPOSING EFFICIENTLY 34

Composing Under Normal Circumstances 36
Composing Under Special Circumstances 44

III

WRITING: MACRO ISSUES 50

Document Design for "High Skim Value" 52
Signposts to Show Connection 60
Effective Paragraphs or Sections 64

IV

WRITING: MICRO ISSUES 68

Editing for Brevity 70
Choosing a Style 76
Writing Checklists 84

V

SPEAKING: VERBAL STRUCTURE **86**

Tell/Sell Presentations 88
Questions and Answers 93
Consult/Join Meetings 97
Other Speaking Situations 102

VI

SPEAKING: VISUAL AIDS **108**

Designing the Presentation as a Whole 110
Designing Each Individual Slide 118
Choosing Visual Aid Equipment 130
Practicing with Visual Aids 132

VII

SPEAKING: NONVERBAL SKILLS **138**

Nonverbal Delivery Skills 140
Nonverbal Listening Skills 152

Speaking Checklists 156

APPENDICES

Appendix A: Formats for Memos, Reports, and Letters 158
Appendix B: Unbiased Language 166
Appendix C: Grammar and Usage 167
Appendix D: Punctuation 173

BIBLIOGRAPHY **179**

INDEX **183**

Introduction

HOW THIS BOOK CAN HELP YOU

If you are facing a specific managerial communication problem, turn to the relevant part of this book for guidance. For example:

- You're speaking or writing to a new group of people. How can you enhance your credibility? How can you persuade them?
- Writing takes you a painfully long time. How can you write faster?
- The thought of giving that presentation next week is making you nervous. What can you do to relax?
- People are not responding to your emails. How can you make them more effective?
- Your new computer software can create terrific visual aids and writing formats. How can you get the most out of them?
- Your boss is returning your memos and reports to you to rewrite. How can you organize your ideas? How can you express yourself more succinctly?
- You're facilitating an important meeting or videoconference next month. How should you prepare for it?

If you don't have a specific question, but need general guidelines, procedures, and techniques, read through this entire book. For example:

- You would like a framework for thinking strategically about all managerial communication.

- You would like to know more about the process of writing and editing more efficiently.
- You would like a step-by-step procedure for preparing an oral presentation or meeting.

If you are taking a professional training course, a college course, a workshop, or a seminar, use this book as a reference.

- You may very well be a good communicator already. You would like, however, to polish and refine your managerial writing and speaking skills by taking a course or seminar.

WHO CAN USE THIS BOOK

This book is written for you if you need to speak or write in a managerial, business, government, or professional context—that is, if you need to achieve results with and through other people. You probably already know these facts:

- *You spend most of your time at work communicating.* Various studies show that 50 to 90 percent of work time is spent in some communication task.
- *Your success is based on communication.* Other studies verify that your career advancement is correlated with your ability to communicate well.
- *Communication is increasingly important today.* Recent trends—such as increased globalization, technology, and specialization—make persuasive communication more crucial than ever.

WHY THIS BOOK WAS WRITTEN

The thousands of participants in various business and professional speaking and writing courses I have taught want a brief summary of communication techniques. Many busy professionals have found other books on communication skills too long, insultingly remedial, or full of irrelevant information.

This book is appropriate for you if you want a guide that is short, professional, and readable.

- *Short:* The book summarizes results and models culled from thousands of pages of text and research. I have omitted bulky examples, cases, footnotes, and exercises.
- *Professional:* This book includes only information that professionals will find useful. You will not find instructions for study skills, such as in-class writing and testing; secretarial skills, such as typing letters and answering telephones; artistic skills, such as writing dialogue and performing dramatic readings; or job-seeking skills, such as résumé writing and job interviewing.
- *Readable:* I have tried to make the book clear and practical. The format makes it easy to read and to skim. The tone is direct, matter-of-fact, and nontheoretical.

HOW THIS BOOK IS ORGANIZED

The book is divided into four main sections.

Communication strategy (Chapter I)

Effective managerial communication—written or oral—is based on an effective strategy. Therefore, you should analyze the five strategic variables covered in this chapter before you start to write or speak: (1) communicator strategy (objectives, style, and credibility); (2) audience strategy (who they are, what they know, what they feel, and how you can persuade them); (3) message strategy (how to emphasize and organize); (4) channel choice strategy (when to write and when to speak); and (5) culture strategy (how cultural differences affect your strategy).

Writing (Chapters II, III, IV, and Appendices)

Chapter II offers techniques on the writing process—that is, how to write faster. Chapter III deals with "macro," or larger, issues in writing—including document design, signposts to show connection, and paragraphs or sections. Chapter IV covers "micro," or smaller, writing issues—including editing for brevity and choosing a style. The appendices cover writing formats, grammar, and punctuation.

Speaking (Chapters V, VI, and VII)

The speaking section discusses three aspects of business speaking. Chapter V explains the verbal aspects—that is, what you say—in presentations, question-and-answer sessions, meetings, and other speaking situations. Chapter VI describes visual aids, including design, equipment, and practice. Chapter VII analyzes nonverbal delivery and listening skills.

Reference

The last section of the book contains appendices that deal with business writing formats, inclusive language, grammar, and punctuation. Finally, the bibliography lists my sources.

ACKNOWLEDGMENTS

I offer grateful acknowledgment to the many people who helped make this book possible. Thanks to my reviewers: June Ferrill (Rice University), Janis Forman (UCLA's Anderson School), Neal Hartman (MIT's Sloan School), Bill Kohler (University of Illinois, Chicago), Charlotte Rosen (Cornell's Johnson School), and Bob Stowers (College of William & Mary). Thanks also to my colleagues Lynn Russell and JoAnne Yates. And, of course, all my love and respect goes to the Admiral.

Over the past 30 years, I have been privileged to work with excellent colleagues, executives, and students. My thanks to colleagues from the Managerial Communication Association and the Association for Business Communication. Thanks also to the thousands of executives from more than 90 companies for their "real-world" experience and insights. I can scarcely believe that I have now taught literally thousands of students—at Dartmouth's Tuck School of Business, Stanford Graduate School of Business, and several international universities. To them, I offer my thanks for their challenges and ideas. Finally, I would like to acknowledge my sources listed in the bibliography.

Mary Munter
Tuck School of Business, Dartmouth College
mary.munter@dartmouth.edu

Guide to

Managerial Communication

Effective Business Writing and Speaking

CHAPTER I OUTLINE

I. Communicator strategy
   1. What is your objective?
   2. What communication style do you choose?
   3. What is your credibility?

II. Audience strategy
   1. Who are they?
   2. What do they know?
   3. What do they feel?
   4. How can you persuade them?

III. Message strategy
   1. How can you emphasize?
   2. How can you organize?

IV. Channel choice strategy
   1. Writing
   2. Speaking to a group (face-to-face)
   3. Speaking to a group (electronically)
   4. Speaking to an individual

V. Culture strategy

CHAPTER I

Communication Strategy

Managerial communication is different from other kinds of communication. Why? Because in a business or management setting, a brilliant message alone is not sufficient: you are successful only if your message results in your desired response from your audience. Therefore, instead of thinking of communication as a straight line from a sender to a receiver, visualize communication as a circle, as shown below, with your success based on achieving your desired response.

To get that desired audience response, you need to think strategically about your communication—before you start to write or speak. Strategic communication is based on five interactive variables: (1) communicator (the writer or speaker) strategy, (2) audience strategy, (3) the message strategy, (4) channel choice strategy, and (5) cultural context strategy. These variables may affect one another; for example, your audience analysis affects your communicator style, your channel choice may affect your message, and the cultural context may affect your channel choice.

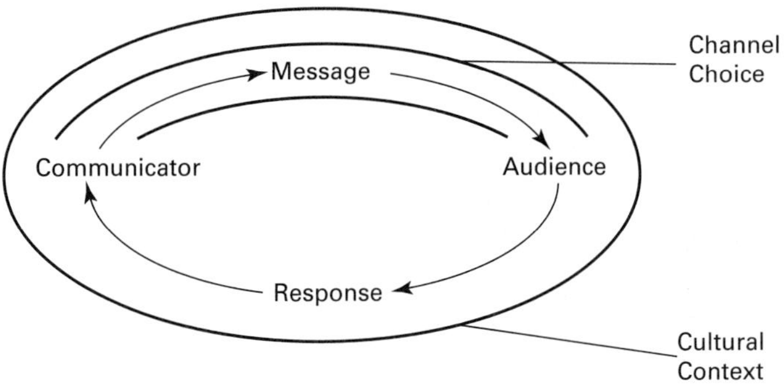

I. COMMUNICATOR STRATEGY

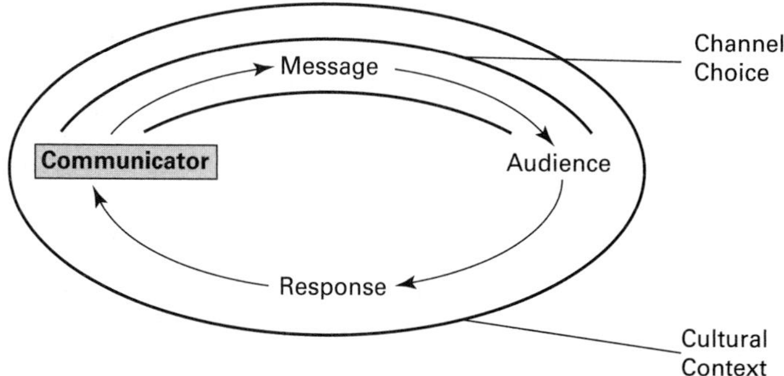

One element of your communication strategy has to do with a set of issues involving you, the communicator. Regardless of whether you are speaking or writing, your communicator strategy includes your objectives, style, and credibility.

1. What is your objective?

It's easy to communicate and receive a random response from your audience—because their response might be to ignore, misunderstand, or disagree with you. However, effective strategic communicators are those who receive their desired response or desired outcome. To clarify this outcome, hone your thoughts from the general to the specific.

General objective This is your broad overall goal, toward which each separate communication will aim.

Action objectives Then, break down your general goal into a consciously planned series of action outcomes—specific, measurable, time-bound steps that will lead toward your general objectives. State your action objectives in this form: "To accomplish a specific result by a specific time."

Communication objective Your communication objective is even more specific. It is focused on the result you hope to achieve from a single communication effort (or episode)—such as a report, email, or presentation. To create a communication objective, start with the phrase: "As a result of this communication, my audience will . . ." Then complete the statement by identifying precisely what you want your audience to do, know, or think as a result of having read or heard your communication.

EXAMPLES OF OBJECTIVES		
General	**Action**	**Communication**
Update management on department performance.	Report two times each quarter.	As a result of this presentation, my boss will learn the results of two new HR programs.
Increase customer base.	Sign with 20 new clients each month.	As a result of this letter, the client will sign and return the contract.
Develop a sound financial position.	Maintain annual debt-to-equity ratio no greater than X.	As a result of this email, the accountant will give me the quarterly expense information for my report. As a result of this report, the board will approve my recommendations.
Increase the number of women hired.	Hire 15 women by March 31, 2007.	As a result of this meeting, we will come up with a strategy to accomplish our goal. As a result of this presentation, at least 10 women will sign up to interview with my firm.
Maintain market share.	Sell X amount by X date.	As a result of this memo, my boss will approve my marketing plan. As a result of this presentation, the sales representatives will understand the three new product enhancements.

2. What communication style do you choose?

As you define your communication objective, choose the appropriate style to reach that objective. The following framework, adapted from Tannenbaum and Schmidt, displays the range of communication styles used in virtually everyone's job at various times. Instead of trying to find one "right" style, use the appropriate style at the appropriate time and avoid using the same style all of the time.

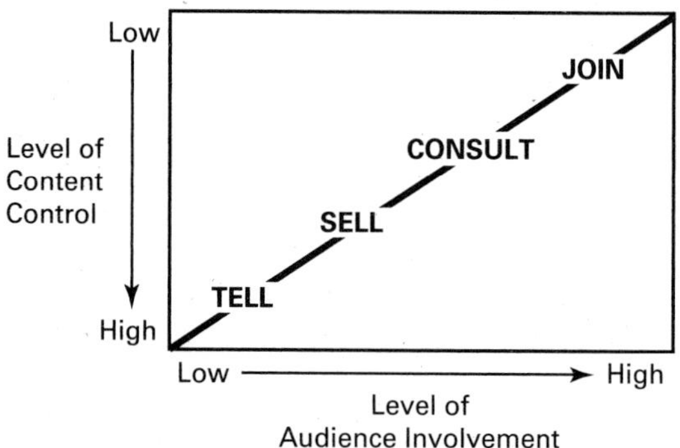

When to use the tell/sell style Use the tell/sell style when you want your audience to learn from you. In the *tell* style, you are informing or explaining; you want your audience to understand something you already know. In the *sell* style, you are persuading or advocating; you want your audience to change their thinking or behavior. In tell/sell situations:

- You have sufficient information.
- You do not need to hear others' opinions, ideas, or input.
- You want to control the message content.

When to use the consult/join style Use the consult/join style, sometimes called the "inquiry style," when you want to learn from the audience. The *consult* style is somewhat collaborative (like a questionnaire); the *join* style is even more collaborative (like a brainstorming session). In consult/join situations:

- You do not have sufficient information.
- You need to or want to understand others' opinions, ideas, or input.
- You need to or want to involve your audience, coming up with message content together.

When to use a combination of styles In an ongoing communication project, you may need to use a combination of styles: for example, *join* to brainstorm ideas, *consult* to choose one of those ideas, *sell* to persuade your boss to adopt that idea, and *tell* to write up the idea once it becomes policy.

EXAMPLES OF OBJECTIVES AND STYLES

Communication Objective	Communication Style
As a result of reading this memo, the employees will be able to compare and contrast the three benefits programs available in this company. As a result of this presentation, my boss will learn the seven major accomplishments of our department this month.	**TELL:** In these situations, you are instructing or explaining. You want your audience to learn, to understand. You do not need your audience's opinions.
As a result of reading this letter, my client will sign the enclosed contract. As a result of this presentation, the committee will approve my proposed budget.	**SELL:** In these situations, you are persuading or advocating. You want your audience to do something different. You need some audience involvement to get them to do so.
As a result of reading this cover letter, the employees will respond by answering the questionnaire. As a result of this question-and-answer session, my staff will voice and obtain replies to their concerns about the new vacation policy.	**CONSULT:** In these situations, you are conferring. You need some give-and-take with your audience. You want to learn from them, yet control the interaction somewhat.
As a result of reading this agenda memo, the group will come to the meeting prepared to offer their thoughts on this specific issue. As a result of this brainstorming session, the group will come up with a solution to this specific problem.	**JOIN:** In these situations, you are collaborating. You and your audience are working together to come up with the content.

3. What is your credibility?

Another aspect of communicator strategy involves analyzing your audience's perception of you. In other words, consider your own credibility: your audience's belief, confidence, and faith in you. Their perception of you has a tremendous impact on how you should communicate with them.

Five factors (based on social power theorists French, Raven, and Kotter) affect your credibility: (1) rank, (2) goodwill, (3) expertise, (4) image, and (5) common ground. Once you understand these factors, you can enhance your credibility by stressing your initial credibility and by increasing your acquired credibility.

Initial credibility Initial credibility refers to your audience's perception of you before you even begin to communicate, before they ever read or hear what you have to say. Your initial credibility, then, may stem from their perception of who you are, what you represent, or how you have related to them previously.

As part of your communication strategy, you may want to stress or remind your audience of the grounds for your initial credibility. Also, in those lucky situations in which your initial credibility is high, you may use it as a "bank account." If people in your audience regard you highly, they may trust you even in unpopular or extreme decisions or recommendations. Just as drawing on a bank account reduces your bank balance, however, drawing on your initial credibility reduces your credibility balance; you must "deposit" more to your account, perhaps by goodwill gestures or further proof of your expertise.

Acquired credibility In contrast, acquired credibility refers to your audience's perception of you after the communication has taken place, after they have read or heard what you have to say. Even if your audience knows nothing about you in advance, your good ideas and your persuasive writing or speaking will help earn you credibility. The obvious way to heighten your credibility, therefore, is to do a good job of communicating.

You might also want to associate yourself with a high-credibility person, acknowledge values you share with your audience, or use any of the other techniques listed on the chart on the facing page.

FACTORS AND TECHNIQUES FOR CREDIBILITY			
Factor	**Based on . . .**	**Stress initial credibility by . . .**	**Increase acquired credibility by . . .**
Rank	Hierarchical power	Emphasizing your title or rank	Associating yourself with or citing a high-ranking person (e.g., by his or her cover letter or introduction)
Goodwill	Personal relationship or "track record"	Referring to relationship or "track record"	Building your goodwill by emphasizing audience benefits, "what's in it for them"
	Trustworthiness	Offering balanced evaluation; acknowledging any conflict of interest	
Expertise	Knowledge, competence	Sharing your expert understanding Explaining how you gained your expertise	Associating yourself with or citing authoritative sources
Image	Attractiveness, audience desire to be like you	Emphasizing attributes audience finds attractive	Building your image by identifying yourself with your audience's benefits; using nonverbals and language your audience considers dynamic
Common ground	Common values, ideas, problems, or needs	Establishing your shared values or ideas Acknowledging similarities with audience Tying the message to your common ground	

II. AUDIENCE STRATEGY

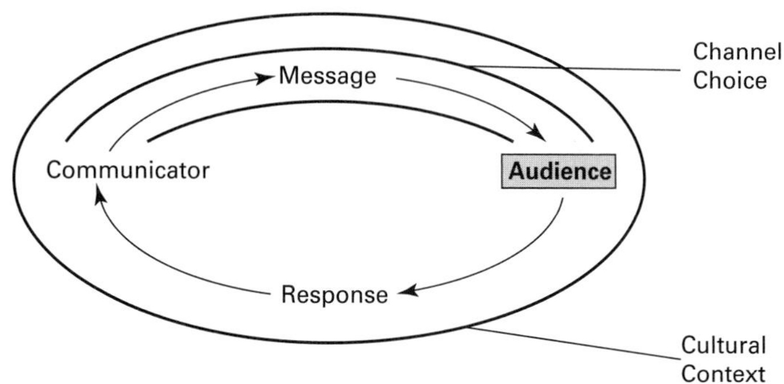

Audience strategy—that is, techniques for gearing your communication toward your audience's needs and interests—is possibly the most important aspect of your communication strategy, because it has the most effect on increasing your chances of being understood and of achieving your objective. Some communication experts recommend performing your audience analysis first; others recommend performing your communicator strategy first. All experts agree, however, that the two strategies interact with and affect one another. So, perhaps the best idea is to perform these analyses concurrently.

Audience strategy includes answering four sets of questions: (1) Who are they? (2) What do they know? (3) What do they feel? (4) How can you persuade them?

1. Who are they?

"Who are they?" sounds like a fairly straightforward question, yet choosing the people to include and focus on is often subtle and complex. To decide whom to include and how to analyze them, answer the following four questions.

Who are the key influencers? Who has the most direct power or influence over the outcome of the communication? Who has indirect influence (opinion leaders, potential allies, or "gatekeepers" from whom you need approval or routing)?

Who should be included in your audience? Based on your analysis of the key influencers, decide who should be included in your audience.

- *Primary audience* will actually receive your message directly.
- *Secondary audiences* will receive your message indirectly—such as receiving a copy, approving in advance, or otherwise influencing the outcome. Sometimes your secondary audience may be more important than your primary audience.

What should you find out? The more you can learn about your audience—both as individuals and as a group—the more likely you are to achieve your desired outcome from them. Find out about:

- *Demographic issues,* such as age range, education, occupation, socioeconomic status, ethnic origin, gender, culture, and language fluency
- *Knowledge and beliefs,* such as their backgrounds, opinions, and values
- *Preferences,* such as style, channel, and format

How can you find out about them? Given your time constraints and relationship with the audience, learn as much about them as possible.

- *Find any market research,* Internet, or other public data that's available.
- *Talk to audience members* in advance or ask someone who knows them.
- *Reflect* on your past impressions or empathize with them.
- *Keep collecting audience information* throughout your communication project, based on their reactions and questions.

2. What do they know?

Next, think about what the audience knows and what they need to know. More specifically, ask yourself these three questions.

How much background information do they need? What do they already know about the topic? How much jargon will they understand?

- *Low background needs:* If their background information needs are low, don't waste their time with unnecessary background or definitions.
- *High background needs:* If their background information needs are high, be sure to define new terms or jargon, link new information to information they already know, and use an extremely clear structure.
- *Mixed background needs:* With mixed audiences, put background information in a separate appendix or handout, or gear the communication toward the key decision maker.

How much new information do they need? What do they need to learn about the topic? How much detail and evidence do they need?

- *High information needs:* If they need it, provide sufficient evidence, statistics, data, and other material. Do they need the sources documented? If so, are the sources credible to them?
- *Low information needs:* On the other hand, many times they don't need a lot of new information: for example, they may trust your expert opinion or delegate the decision to you. Think in terms of how much information your audience needs, not how much information you can possibly provide.
- *Mixed information needs:* With mixed audiences, put additional detail in a separate appendix or handout, or gear the communication toward the key decision maker.

What are their expectations and preferences? What do they expect or prefer in terms of style, channel, or format?

- *Style preferences:* What, if anything, do they expect in terms of cultural, organizational, or personal style—such as formal or informal, straightforward or indirect, interactive or noninteractive, stringent timing or flexible timing?
- *Channel preferences:* What, if anything, do they expect in terms of channel choice—such as hard copy versus email, group versus individual meetings, or handouts versus slides?
- *Standard length and format preferences:* What, if anything, do they expect in terms of standard document or presentation length or format—such as a standard format for one-page memos or standard half-hour weekly informal meetings?

3. What do they feel?

Remember, your audience's emotional level is just as important as their knowledge level. Therefore, in addition to thinking about what they know, think about what they feel. Answering the following questions will give you a sense of the emotions your audience may be bringing to the communication.

What emotions do they feel? What feelings may arise from their current situation or their emotional attitude?

- *What is their current situation?* Is there anything about the economic situation, the timing, or their morale that you should keep in mind?
- *What emotions might they feel about your message?* Many communicators mistakenly think that all business audiences are driven by facts and rationality alone. In truth, they may also be driven by their feelings about your message: they may feel positive emotions (such as pride, excitement, and hope), or negative ones (such as anxiety, fear, or jealousy).

How interested are they in your message? Is your message a high priority or low priority for your audience? How likely are they to choose to read what you write or to listen carefully to what you say? How curious are they and how much do they care about the issue or its outcomes?

- *High interest level:* If their interest level is high, you can get right to the point without taking much time to arouse their interest. Build a good logical argument. Do not expect a change of opinion without continued effort over time; however, if you can persuade them, their change will be more permanent than changes in a low-interest audience.
- *Low interest level:* If, on the other hand, their interest level is low, think about using a consult/join style and ask them to participate: one of the strongest ways to build support is to share control. If, however, you are using a tell/sell style, use one or more of the techniques discussed on pages 15–17 to persuade them. In addition, keep your message as short as possible; long documents are intimidating and listeners tune out anything that seems like rambling. Finally, for low-interest audiences, act quickly on attitude changes because they may not be permanent.

What is their probable bias: positive or negative? What is their probable attitude toward your ideas or recommendations? Are they likely to favor them, be indifferent, or be opposed? What do they have to gain or lose from your ideas? Why might they say "no"?

- *Positive or neutral:* If they are positive or neutral, reinforce their existing attitude by stating the benefits that will accrue from your message.
- *Negative:* If they are negative, try one or more of these techniques: (1) Convince them that there is a problem, then solve the problem. (2) State points with which you think they will agree first; if audience members are sold on two or three key features of your proposal, they will tend to sell themselves on the other features as well. (3) Limit your request to the smallest one possible, such as a pilot program rather than a full program right away. (4) Respond to anticipated objections; you will be more persuasive by stating and rejecting alternatives yourself, instead of allowing them to devise their own, which they will be less likely to reject.

Is your desired action easy or hard for them? From their perspective, what will your communication objective entail in terms of their immediate task? Will it be time-consuming, complicated, or difficult for them?

- *Easy or hard for them:* Whether your desired action is easy or hard, always show how it supports the audience's beliefs or benefits them.
- *Hard for them:* If it is hard, try one of these techniques: (1) Break the action down into the smallest possible request, such as a signature approving an idea that someone else is lined up to implement. (2) Make the action as easy as you can, such as distributing a questionnaire that they can fill in easily or providing them with a checklist they can follow easily.

4. How can you persuade them?

Of the following three sets of persuasion techniques, choose those that will work best for your particular audience.

Persuade by using audience benefits. Stress "what's in it for them."

- *Tangible benefits:* Sometimes you will be able to highlight tangible benefits that you can offer your audience. Emphasize their value (for example, profits, savings, bonuses, or product discounts), significance as symbols (for example, offices, furnishings, or jewelry), or uniqueness and exclusiveness. Effective tangible benefits do not need to be elegant. Items such as T-shirts, mugs, or pens will work effectively—if they are valued by the audience.
- *Career or task benefits:* (1) Sometimes you can persuade by showing how your message will enhance your audience's job—by solving a current problem, saving them time, or making their job easier or more convenient. (2) Or you can appeal to the task itself. Some audiences may appreciate the chance to be challenged, or to participate in tough problem solving or decision making. (3) Other people respond to appeals to their career advancement or prestige. Let them know how they will win organizational recognition, enhance their reputation, or develop networking contacts.
- *Ego benefits:* For some audiences, persuade by enhancing their sense of self-worth, accomplishment, and achievement. For example, show them they are accepted and included by soliciting their suggestions or inviting them to participate. You can incorporate emotional support into your communication with informal verbal praise or with nonverbal smiles and nods with more formal statements.
- *Personality benefits:* Different personalities are persuaded differently. For example, persuade thinkers with lots of data, skeptics with lots of credibility, unemotional people with rationality, and emotional people with enthusiasm and energy.
- *Group benefits:* For group-oriented audiences, emphasize benefits to the group as a whole: appeal to any tangible group benefits, group task enhancements, group advancements, or sense of group worth. For audiences who value solidarity with the group, use statements of group consensus or coalition rather than expert testimony or your individual credibility. For people who are strongly influenced by the beliefs and actions of those around them, use the "bandwagon" technique. In the words of communication expert JoAnne Yates, "Although the fact that 'everyone is doing it' may not be a very good logical argument, it nevertheless influences some people."

Persuade by using credibility. On pages 8–9, we discussed various factors that influence your credibility. Here are some techniques to apply your credibility as a persuasive tool. Remember, the less your audience is involved in the topic or issue, the more important your credibility is as a factor for persuasion.

- *Shared values credibility and "common ground":* Establishing a common ground with your audience is highly persuasive, especially when done at the beginning of your message. For example, refer to goals you share with your audience before focusing on your controversial recommendation to achieve them.
- *Goodwill credibility and "reciprocity":* A persuasive technique for applying goodwill credibilty is through "reciprocity" or "bargaining." People generally feel obliged to reciprocate gifts, favors, and concessions—even uninvited or unwanted ones. So, you might gain a favor by granting a favor; you might offer a concession to gain a concession.
- *Goodwill credibility and "liking":* People tend to be more persuaded by people they like. So, taking the time to meet your audience one-to-one, to establish a relationship, to uncover real similarities, and to offer genuine praise will make you more persuasive in the long run.
- *Image credibility and emotionality:* Another way to persuade is to connect emotionally with your audience. Show your emotional commitment and adjust your emotions to your audience's emotional state.
- *Rank and expertise credibility by association:* Sometimes, rank and expertise can be persuasive. So, either refer to your own rank or expertise, or else use rank or expertise by association (for example, have the CEO introduce you or cite credible experts).
- *Rank credibility and punishment:* The most extreme application of rank credibility is using threats and punishments, such as reprimands, pay cuts, demotions, or even dismissal. Researchers have found that threats produce tension, provoke counteraggression, increase fear and dislike, work only when you're on the spot to assure compliance, and may eliminate an undesired behavior without producing the desired behavior. Therefore, threats and punishments are inappropriate for most audiences and most situations.

Persuade by using message structure. Finally, in some situations, you might motivate your audience by the way you structure your message.

- *Opening and closing:* Emphasize audience benefits in your opening and closing.
- *The problem/solution structure:* If you can convince your audience that there is a problem, then according to "balance theory" (or the "consistency principle"), they will feel out of balance and want to come back to equilibrium by accepting your solution.
- *One-sided or two-sided structure:* Use a two-sided approach for a major or controversial subject, a sophisticated or negative audience, or an audience who will hear opposing arguments. This technique works because (1) they will hear your positive arguments more clearly after their concerns have been addressed, (2) they are more likely to reject alternatives explained to them than alternatives they bring up themselves, and (3) you will appear more reasonable and fair-minded. Use a one-sided argument for an uninformed or neutral audience.
- *Pro/con or con/pro:* List the "pros" first for a noncontroversial subject or if your credibility is high; list the "cons" first for a delicate, highly charged situation or if your credibility is low.
- *Ascending or descending order:* Use an ascending order (strongest arguments first) with an informed or interested audience; use a descending order for a less informed or engaged audience.
- *The "ask for less" (or "foot in door") technique:* If you break down your communication objective into the smallest possible request, one that you are likely to get (such as a pilot program), then later you will be more likely to get the larger request. Similarly, make it easy for the audience to respond: for example, provide a survey they can fill in easily, a checklist they can follow, or specific next steps or specific actions.
- *The "ask for more" (or "door in face") technique:* The opposite of "ask for less" is to ask for an extreme request that you fully expect to be rejected, followed by a more moderate request that is more likely to be honored.

You can also persuade by using the additional message strategies covered in the next section.

III. MESSAGE STRATEGY

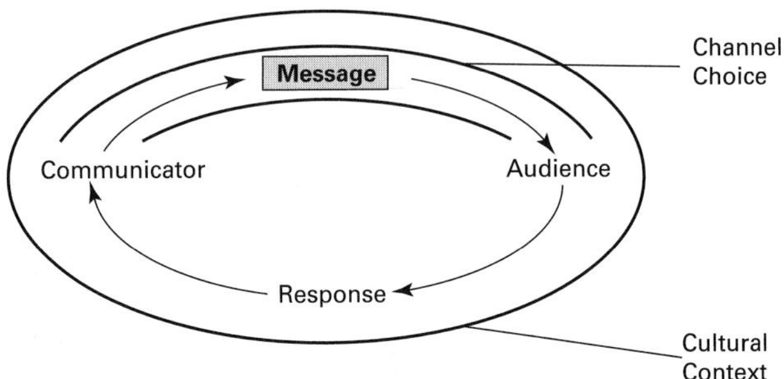

Structuring your message is a third variable in your communication strategy. Ineffective communicators simply state their ideas in the order they happen to occur to them; effective communicators use structure strategically. When you think, all kinds of ideas occur to you—some good, some bad, some complete, some fragmented; the end result of the thought process is your conclusion. But you don't want your audience to have to wade through all the false starts and disjointed ideas you went through during the thought process, so when you communicate strategically, you emphasize and organize your ideas clearly for your audience. The following illustration graphically demonstrates this difference:

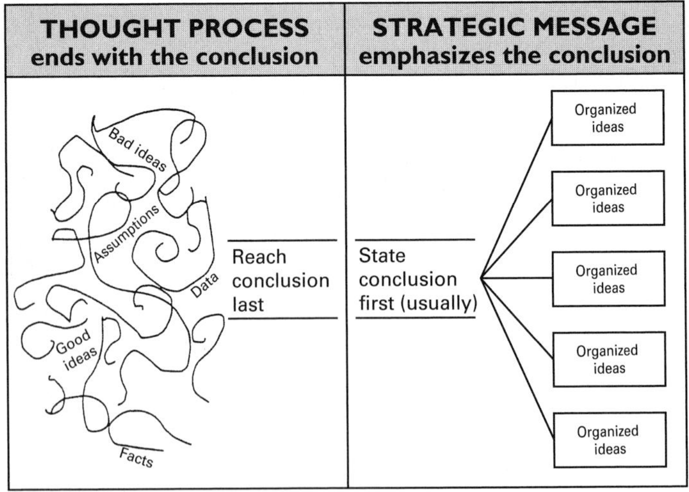

Instead of structuring your message as ideas happen to occur to you, ask the following questions: (1) How can you emphasize? (2) How can you organize?

1. How can you emphasize?

The Audience Memory Curve, illustrated here, summarizes research on what your audience is most likely to remember from your message.

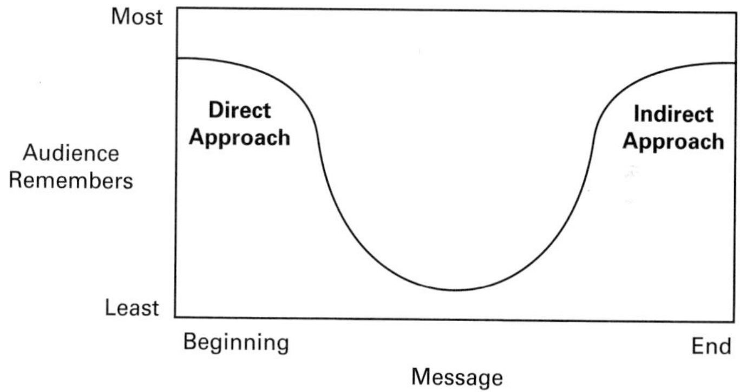

What does the Audience Memory Curve imply? First, that you should never bury important ideas in the middle of your message. Second, that you need to keep your audience's attention throughout by using the persuasion techniques described on pages 15–17. Third, that your opening or introduction is extremely important. Finally, that you should state your important ideas prominently—either at the beginning or at the end (or both).

Stating your main ideas first is called the direct approach; stating them last is called the indirect approach.

Using the direct approach The direct approach, stating your main ideas at the beginning of your message, is sometimes called "bottom-lining" your message, because you state the bottom line first. For example,

> The committee recommends policy x for the following reasons:
>
> Reason 1
>
> Reason 2
>
> Reason 3

Advantages of the direct approach Using the direct approach has many advantages.

- *Improves comprehension:* People assimilate and comprehend content more easily when they know the conclusions first. Withholding your conclusion until the end is fine for a mystery story, but not for busy business audiences who may resent every minute they spend trying to figure out what you're attempting to communicate.
- *Is audience-centered:* The direct approach emphasizes the results of your analysis. In contrast, the indirect approach is communicator-centered because it mirrors the steps you went through to formulate your conclusions.
- *Saves time:* The direct approach saves your audience time. They can understand the message with little rereading or repetition, and they can decide immediately which sections they can skim, read carefully, or use as reference.

Why the direct approach is underutilized Why, then, do people often avoid the direct approach?

- *Habit:* For one thing, communicators find it is easier to write or speak the way they think, even though it is harder on their readers or listeners.
- *Academic training:* Many communicators have been reinforced in the use of indirect structure throughout years of schooling.
- *Suspense:* Some communicators think the indirect strategy will build suspense and keep their audience's attention. In fact, however, it merely befuddles them.
- *Effort:* Finally, some people want their audience to appreciate all the effort they went through, when, in fact, such an approach may lead to unnecessary confusion rather than understanding.

When to use the direct approach Because the direct approach is easier and faster to follow, you should use it as much as possible in Anglo-American business situations, probably about 90% of the time. (See pages 29–31 for more on cultural differences.) Specifically, use the direct approach for:

- All nonsensitive messages, that is, those with no emotional overtones
- Sensitive messages if the audience's bias is positive
- Sensitive messages if the audience is results-oriented
- Sensitive messages if your credibility is particularly high

Using the indirect approach An indirect approach, saving your main idea until the end of your message, involves spelling out your support first, then finishing with your generalization or conclusion. Indirect structure is sometimes called the "mystery story approach." For example,

Reason 1

Reason 2

Reason 3

Therefore, the committee recommends policy x.

When to use the indirect approach Because this approach is hard to follow, takes longer for your audience to understand, and does not take advantage of the audience's attentiveness at the beginning of the message, use it only when the following conditions apply:

- Cultural norms so dictate
- Your message is sensitive (with emotional overtones)
- Your audience's bias is negative
- Your audience is analysis-oriented
- Your credibility is low

Advantages of the indirect approach When these conditions apply, the indirect strategy may soften your audience's resistance, arouse their interest, and increase their tendency to see you as fair-minded. Also, the indirect approach gives you the chance to let your audience "buy into" ideas they agree with or a problem they need to solve, before you present your solution.

2. How can you organize?

Once you have emphasized your main idea by placing it first (direct approach) or last (indirect approach), organize your supporting points accordingly.

EXAMPLES OF STRATEGIC MESSAGES

Communication objective	If it is a . . .	Then, use this approach . . .	And organize by . . .
Staff will follow procedure.	Routine procedure	Direct	Listing the steps in the procedure
	New procedure, hostile audience	Indirect	Discussing the benefits of procedure, followed by steps in procedure
Boss will approve plan.	Busy audience, or your credibility high	Direct	Explaining the plan, then the reasons why
	Audience is analysis-oriented, and your credibility low	Indirect	Listing the supporting reasons, then the plan
Customer will purchase our service.	Audience is results-oriented, or bias is indifferent	Direct	Recommending your service, followed by audience benefits from service
	Audience bias is negative	Indirect	Listing the benefits from your service and/or problems with competitor's service, then recommend your service

IV. CHANNEL CHOICE STRATEGY

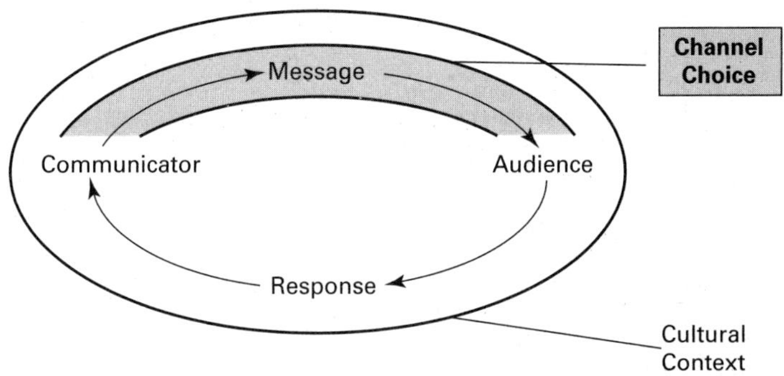

Channel choice refers to the choice of medium through which you send your message. In the past, this strategic choice was basically between two channels: writing and speaking. Today, many more channels exist—including fax, email, voicemail, electronic meetings, and videoteleconferencing. These new channels have changed how we think about channel choice. For example, traditional writing is usually fairly reserved and controlled; email, however, may be informal and spontaneous. Before you choose a channel from among this expanded set of alternatives, think about these general questions. Do you need to:

- *Be formal or informal?* Both writing and speaking can be either formal or informal—for example, formal reports or informal emails, formal presentations or informal meetings.
- *Receive an immediate response* and have control over whether your message is received or not?
- *Elicit high audience participation or not?* Face-to-face or not?
- *Have a "rich" communication or not?* Text only is the least rich channel; text plus pictures plus voice plus body language is the most rich channel.
- *Have a permanent record or not?* Retransmit easily or not?
- *Use a channel preferred by your audience* or their culture?

Once you have considered these general issues, choose from among the following options, weighing the advantages and disadvantages of each. If you do not have your choice of channels, think about how you can utilize the advantages of, and overcome the disadvantages of, the channel you need to use.

I. Writing

Writing channels include traditional writing, fax, email, and web page.

Traditional writing

- *Advantages of traditional writing:* Choose writing when you want to (1) use precise wording and grammar, because you can edit; (2) include a great deal of detail, because readers can assimilate more detail than listeners; (3) save time for your audience, because reading is faster than listening; (4) enable your reader to focus on certain sections of interest; (5) have a private communication; (6) reach a geographically dispersed audience; (7) have a permanent and accessible record.
- *Disadvantages of traditional writing:* If you write, you will have (1) delayed transmission time, (2) no control over if or when the message is received or who else might read it, (3) a delayed response, if any, (4) no nonverbal communication, (5) possible lack of flexibility and too much rigidity.

Facsimile (fax)

- *Advantages:* Same as traditional writing, but with faster transmission time; can "blast fax" to multiple audiences simultaneously.
- *Disadvantages:* Same as traditional writing, but usually less private; may not reproduce graphics precisely.

Electronic mail (email)

- *Advantages:* Same as traditional writing, plus (1) less likely to be inhibited and reserved, at best, more likely to be spontaneous and creative; (2) less likely to take much preparation time; (3) more likely to contact people in all levels of an organization; (4) more likely to include written nonverbal cues by using "emoticons," such as :-) :-(; (5) easy for audience to respond quickly; (6) can "blast email" to multiple audiences simultaneously.
- *Disadvantages:* (1) May be inappropriately uninhibited or irresponsible, at worst, destructive (known as "flaming"); (2) may be hard to read because less likely to edit, full of typos and mistakes, and, more importantly, lack of logical frameworks for the reader—such as headings and transitions; (3) may be useful for short messages only; (4) cannot ever be erased or shredded, becomes property of the company, may be used in lawsuits; (5) may be sent to the wrong person by mistake and irretrievably, forwarded without your permission, sent to too many people unnecessarily; (6) may be a way to avoid confrontation or to avoid consensus building; (7) may be responded to too quickly or mistaken for formal text or formal commitment.

Web page

- *Advantages:* (1) Provides easy access to document at all times, (2) can reach audiences you don't know, (3) allows for self-selected audiences.
- *Disadvantages:* (1) Least personal and private written channel, (2) usually one-way communication, (3) not addressed to specific audience; readers have to look for it.

2. Speaking to a group (face-to-face)

You can speak to a group in a tell/sell or a consult/join style.

Tell/sell presentations

- *Advantages: Compared to writing,* choose presentations when you want to (1) control if and when the message is received and have your audience hear the same information at the same time, (2) receive an immediate and interactive response, (3) include nonverbal communication, (4) build group identity and group relationships. *Compared to meetings,* choose presentations when you want to (1) use the tell or sell styles, (2) do most of the speaking yourself.
- *Disadvantages:* Presentations (1) are less private and confidential than writing, (2) do not provide a permanent and accessible record, (3) require that the audience must be in the same place, (4) do not allow as much detail as writing, because listeners cannot assimilate as much detail as readers, (5) are less precise than writing, because you cannot edit what you say, (6) may be intimidating and speaker-dominated.

Consult/join meetings

- *Advantages: Compared to presentations,* choose meetings when you want to (1) elicit ideas from others, (2) foster group participation and discussion, (3) resolve group issues, (4) receive input from various people or groups, (5) reach a consensus and establish action steps, (6) use consult or join styles. *Compared to electronic meetings,* choose face-to-face meetings when (1) you need the richest nonverbal cues, including body, voice, proximity, and touch; (2) the issues are especially sensitive; (3) the people don't know one another; (4) establishing group rapport and relationships is crucial.
- *Disadvantages: Compared to videoconferences,* face-to-face meetings (1) do not allow the possibility of simultaneous participation in multiple locations, (2) can delay meeting follow-up activities because decisions and action items must be written up after the meeting. *Compared to electronic meetings,* face-to-face meetings (1) may be dominated by overly vocal higher-status participants, (2) may involve high travel costs and time.

3. Speaking to a group (electronically)

Unlike the face-to-face speaking channels discussed previously, the following three channels use different kinds of *groupware*—a broad term for a group of related technologies that mediate group collaboration through technology—that may include any combination of collaborative software or intraware, electronic and voicemail systems, electronic meeting systems, phone systems, video systems, electronic bulletin boards, and group document handling and annotation systems.

Videoconferences

- *Advantages:* Choose videoconferences when (1) the participants are in different places, but you want to communicate with them all at the same time; (2) you want to save on travel time and expenses; (3) you want to inform, explain, or train—as opposed to persuade or sell; (4) you want to collaborate via document sharing.
- *Disadvantages:* (1) They are usually not as effective as face-to-face meetings when you need to persuade or to establish personal relationships; (2) they lack the richest nonverbal cues, such as proximity and touch; (3) fewer people tend to speak and they speak in longer bursts than in other kinds of meetings; (4) they may involve significant set-up time and costs.

Audioconferences Audioconferences are usually called telephone conference calls.

- *Advantages:* Have most of the advantages of videoconferencing, but are (1) cheaper, (2) based on more readily available equipment, (3) less time-consuming and trouble to set up, and (4) less prone to technical glitches.
- *Disadvantages:* Have most of the disadvantages of videoconferencing plus (1) lack of body language makes it harder to interact and to know who is going to speak next, and (2) lack of text or visuals makes it harder to communicate a great deal of detailed information.

Broadcasting or webcasting

- *Advantages:* Can transmit to multiple audiences in multiple locations.
- *Disadvantages:* Usually one-way video, sometimes two-way audio.

Electronic meetings Electronic meeting systems (EMS)—with participants writing on their computers—are *mediated* (that is, they utilize a trained technical facilitator) and usually *synchronous* (that is, everyone participates at the same time).

- *Advantages of EMS:* Choose electronic meetings when you want to (1) generate more ideas and alternatives more quickly than with a traditional note-taker; (2) allow the possibility of anonymous input, which may lead to more candid and truthful replies, equalize participants' status, and increase participation among hierarchical levels; (3) maximize audience participation and in-depth discussion because everyone can "speak" simultaneously, so shy members are more likely to participate and the "vocal few" are less likely to dominate the discussion; (4) provide immediate documentation when meeting is finished.
- *Disadvantages of EMS:* EMS (1) cannot replace face-to-face contact, especially when group efforts are just beginning and when you are trying to build group values, trust, and emotional ties; (2) may exacerbate dysfunctional group dynamics, and increased honesty may lead to increased conflict; (3) may make it harder to reach consensus, because more ideas are generated and because it may be harder to interpret the strength of other members' commitment to their proposals; (4) may demand a good deal of facilitator preparation time and training.

Email meetings Email meetings are *unmediated* (that is, messages go directly to other participants' computers) and *asynchronous* (that is, people respond at their convenience, at different times).

- *Advantages:* At their best, email meetings can (1) increase participation because people can respond when they wish and no scheduling is necessary, (2) speed up meeting follow-up activities because of electronic distribution, (3) decrease transmission time for circulating documents, (4) allow quick discussion and resolution of many small or obscure issues or problems, (5) decrease writing inhibitions with more conversational style than traditional writing, (6) increase communication across hierarchical boundaries.
- *Disadvantages:* At their worst, email meetings can (1) decrease attention to the audience and to social context and regulation; (2) be inappropriately uninhibited or irresponsible, at worst destructive (known as "flaming"); (3) be inappropriately informal; (4) consist of "quick and dirty" messages, with typos and grammatical errors, and, more importantly, lack of logical frameworks for readers—such as headings and transitions; (5) result in a delayed response, or no response; (6) make it harder to gain commitment than with other kinds of meetings.

4. Speaking to an individual

Speak to an individual—not to a group—when you want (1) a private, confidential communication, (2) individual feedback or response, (3) less preparation time, or (4) a fast, simple answer.

Conversation (face-to-face)

- *Advantages:* Compared to email or voicemail, talk with someone face-to-face when (1) you want to build your individual relationship or rapport; (2) the message is especially sensitive or negative; (3) you want a candid, low-risk, fast reply.
- *Disadvantages:* Lacks most of the advantages of writing and speaking to a group plus (1) the person must be located in the same place as you are; (2) if you speak with more than one person, they will hear different information at different times; (3) may be easily misunderstood with no permanent record; (4) may make some people feel excluded.

Telephone

- *Advantages:* (1) Good for candid, low-risk, fast replies; (2) better than face-to-face for reaching people in different places, saves time and travel costs; (3) better than voicemail for establishing rapport.
- *Disadvantages:* (1) Harder to build a personal relationship because fewer nonverbal cues than face-to-face; (2) if you telephone more than one person, they will hear different information at different times.

Voicemail

- *Advantages:* Use voicemail when you want (1) to handle small items quickly; (2) faster distribution than with paper; (3) more emotional content than email, because of nonverbal vocal cues; (4) messages more easily retrieved than email, no computer required; (5) to "blast voicemail" to multiple audiences simultaneously; (6) less likelihood of a permanent record being made; (7) to forward others' vocal messages with your comments.
- *Disadvantages:* (1) Like writing, when you use voicemail, you will have a delayed response, no control over if and when message is received, and no immediate interactivity; (2) like email, voicemail may be forwarded on and distributed widely without your permission; (3) lacks a record; (4) is usually effective for brief messages only; (5) may carry less weight than a document: people may listen to the first part and delete or skip over it entirely.

V. CULTURE STRATEGY

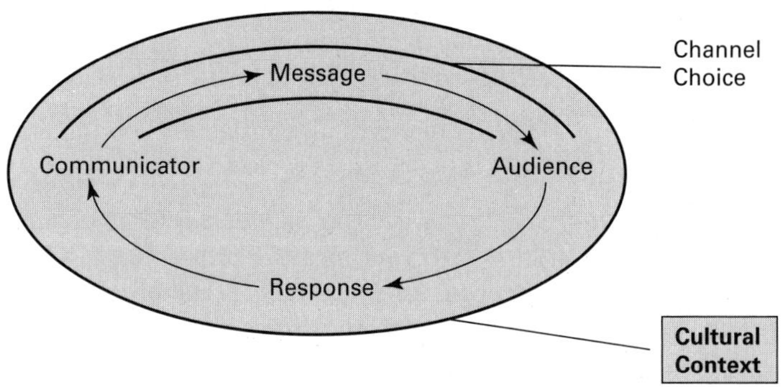

Every aspect of communication strategy we have discussed so far will be greatly influenced by the cultural context in which you are communicating. These cultural differences could result from different countries, regions, industries, organizations, genders, ethnic groups, or work groups. The danger in cultural analysis is stereotyping: saying all the people in a group behave a certain way all the time, and using negative phrasing, such as "all British people are cold." A more useful approach is to think in terms of cultural norms: saying most people in a group behave a certain way most of the time, expressed as a behavior, not as a judgment, such as "the British tend to use formal greetings."

Communicator strategy The culture in which you communicate will affect all three aspects of communicator strategy.

Communication objective Rethink your communication objective in terms of the culture. (1) *Time:* Consider cultural attitudes toward time: you may want to set a different objective in a culture that is relative, relaxed, and tradition-oriented about time than you would in a culture that is precise and future-oriented toward time. (2) *Attitude:* Think also about the cultural attitude toward fate: the objective you set in a culture believing in deterministic fate may be different from one set in a culture believing in human control over fate.

Communication style Different communication styles will tend to work better in different cultures. Group-oriented cultures may favor consult/join styles; individualistic cultures may favor tell/sell styles. Autocratic cultures may favor tell styles; democratic cultures may favor consult styles.

Credibility Different cultures value the five aspects of credibility differently. For instance, goodwill credibility is more important in cultures that value personal relations; expert credibility is more important in cultures that value hard facts and task orientation. Similarly, some cultures value rank, titles, and authority more than others.

Audience strategy The culture will also influence your audience strategy.

Audience selection You may need to include additional primary audiences (people who receive your message directly), and leaders (key decision makers), depending on cultural expectations about rank, authority, and group definition. Also, remember that different cultures have different attitudes toward age, sex, and educational level.

Audience persuasion Different audience persuasion techniques will work more effectively in different cultures. Although some cultures value material wealth and acquisition, others place greater value on work relationships, challenges, or status. Some cultures value Western logic more than others. The relative importance of individual relationships and credibility varies, as does the relative importance of group relationships and identity. Finally, persuasive values and ideals vary tremendously among cultures.

Gender-based tendencies Sometimes it's useful to think about the cultural differences between men and women. Research shows, for example, that men tend to take arguments impersonally, women personally; that men seek quick authoritative decisions, women use consensus building; that men use stronger language even when they're not sure, women use more qualified language even when they are sure; and that men use less active listening, women use more.

Message strategy In addition, cultural factors will influence your choice of message structure. Cultures valuing slow, ritualistic negotiations may favor indirect structure; cultures valuing fast, efficient negotiations may favor direct structure. Authoritarian cultures may favor direct structure downward and indirect structure upward.

Channel strategy Different cultures may have different norms for channel and form—for example, a technical department versus a marketing department or a traditional organization versus a start-up venture. These norms may range from standardized one-page memos to face-to-face hallway discussions. In addition, cultures valuing personal trust more than hard facts tend to prefer oral communication and oral agreements; cultures valuing facts and efficiency tend to prefer written communication and written agreements.

Nonverbal considerations In addition to the other strategic variables we have discussed in this chapter, nonverbal differences present another set of challenges in cross-cultural communication.

Body and voice Consider cultural norms regarding body and voice: posture, gestures, eye contact and direction of gaze, facial expression, touching behaviors, pitch, volume, rate, and attitude toward silence. Avoid gestures considered rude or insulting in that culture; resist applying your own culture's nonverbal meanings to other cultures. For example, Vietnamese may look down to show respect, but that doesn't mean they are "shifty." Northeasterners may speak fast, but that doesn't mean they are "arrogant."

Space and objects Also consider norms regarding space and objects: how much personal space people expect or need, how much institutional space people receive (who works where, with how much space, and with what material objects), how people dress, and how rigid dress codes are. For example, Latin Americans may prefer closer social space; Swedes may prefer more distant social space.

Greetings and hospitality Finally, consider cultural norms regarding greetings and hospitality. Knowing these norms can go a long way toward increasing your rapport and credibility.

For much more on this topic, see the *Guide to Cross-Cultural Communication,* cited on page 180.

Once you have set your communication strategy, then refer to the appropriate chapters:

- ***For writing:*** Chapters II, III, and IV, and the Appendices
- ***For speaking:*** Chapters V, VI, and VII

COMMUNICATION STRATEGY CHECKLIST

Communicator Strategy
See pages 4–9.

1. What is your communication objective: "As a result of this communication, my audience will . . ."?
2. What communication style do you choose: tell, sell, consult, or join?
3. What is your credibility: rank, goodwill, expertise, image, common ground?

Audience Strategy
See pages 10–17.

1. Who are they? Who should be included and how can you find out about them?
2. What do they know: necessary background information and new information; expectations for style, channel, and format?
3. What do they feel: emotions, interest, bias, hard or easy for them?
4. How can you persuade them using audience benefits, credibility, and message structure?

Message Strategy
See pages 18–22.

1. How can you emphasize: direct or indirect?
2. How can you organize a strategic message?

Channel Choice Strategy
See pages 23–28.

1. Writing: traditional, fax, email, or web page?
2. Speaking to a group face-to-face: tell/sell presentation or consult/join meeting?
3. Speaking to a group electronically: videoconference, conference call, broadcast or webcast, electronic meeting, or email meeting?
4. Speaking to an individual: face-to-face, telephone, or voicemail?

Culture Strategy
See pages 29–31.

1. How does the culture affect the communicator strategy: objective, style, credibility?
2. How does the culture affect the audience strategy: selection and persuasion?
3. How does the culture affect the message strategy: direct or indirect?
4. How does the culture affect the channel choice strategy?
5. What nonverbal considerations should you keep in mind?

GUIDE TO THE GUIDE TO MANAGERIAL COMMUNICATION

To set your communication strategy → See Chapter I

- Communicator strategy (objectives, style, and credibility)
- Audience strategy (selection, analysis, and persuasion)
- Message strategy (emphasis and organization)
- Channel choice strategy (write or speak)
- Culture strategy (cultural variables)

If you are writing,

- To enhance the writing process → See Chapter II
  - Compose efficiently
  - Overcome writing problems
- To write effectively on the macro level → See Chapter III
  - Document design
  - Signposts to show connection
  - Paragraphs or sections
- To write effectively on the micro level → See Chapter IV
  - Editing for brevity
  - Editing for style
- To use business formats → See Appendix A
  - Memos, reports, letters
- To write correctly → See Appendices B–D
  - Correct grammar and punctuation

If you are speaking,

- To structure what you say → See Chapter V
  - Tell/sell presentations
  - Questions and answers
  - Consult/join meetings
  - Other situations
- To use effective visual aids → See Chapter VI
  - Overall design
  - Individual slide design
  - Equipment
  - Practice techniques
- To improve your nonverbal delivery skills → See Chapter VII
  - Nonverbal delivery skills
  - Nonverbal listening skills

CHAPTER II OUTLINE

I. Composing under normal circumstances
   1. Gather information
   2. Organize your thoughts
   3. Focus the message
   4. Draft the document
   5. Edit the document

II. Composing under special circumstances
   1. Overcoming writer's block
   2. Using email
   3. Writing in groups

CHAPTER II

Writing: Composing Efficiently

To many business people, writing does not seem as exciting or important as speaking—perhaps because writers are not actually face-to-face with their audience. However, in some ways, writing is more important than speaking because writing is (1) *often a "career sifter"*—that is, a specific report or memo may make or break a promotion or permanent hiring, (2) *permanent* and may be used for or against you long into the future, and (3) *increasingly prevalent* because of word processing and email.

Given its importance, writing (especially email) is all too often tossed off thoughtlessly because business writers are under severe time pressures. Therefore, this chapter concentrates on how to write under time pressure, how to compose more efficiently—that is, faster—(1) under normal circumstances, and (2) under special circumstances—including writer's block, email, and group writing. (Chapter III will deal with the reader's time pressures and how to make your writing easier to read quickly.)

WRITING: COMPOSING EFFICIENTLY		
Section in this chapter:	**I. Composing Under Normal Circumstances**	**II. Composing Under Special Circumstances**
Goal:	To write faster	To overcome special writing challenges

I. COMPOSING UNDER NORMAL CIRCUMSTANCES

WRITING: COMPOSING EFFICIENTLY		
Section in this chapter:	**I. Composing Under Normal Circumstances**	**II. Composing Under Special Circumstances**
Goal:	To write faster	To overcome special writing challenges

Before you sit down and start writing, make some decisions and set some expectations for yourself.

- *Setting your strategy first:* Before you write, always set, review, and keep in mind your communication strategy, as explained in the previous chapter.
- *Deciding whether to write or not:* As a part of that strategy, give some thought to a basic strategic issue: should you write or not? (1) Do you have an important reason to write? (2) Is writing too rigid? Do you want to solidify what may be temporary feelings on the matter? (3) Is writing too risky? Are you sure you want a permanent record? (4) Do you need to see your audience's reactions immediately? (5) Given your audience's situation, is this the right time to be writing? (6) Are you the right person to be writing this document?
- *Differentiating activities:* Once you decide it is appropriate to write, you will be more efficient if you can differentiate the five activities in the writing process: (1) gathering, (2) organizing, (3) focusing, (4) drafting, and (5) editing. Each of these activities calls for different skills.
- *Expecting overlap:* At the same time that you differentiate these stages, do not expect them to occur in lockstep order. Instead, during any one of these stages, be prepared to loop back, to rethink, to make changes. For example, once you've focused your ideas, you may find you need to collect more information for certain topics; or, once you've completed a draft, you may discover you need to reorganize some of your ideas. If you expect this kind of intelligent flexibility, you will take it in stride when the need for it occurs.

A helpful way to visualize the composition process, adopted from writing expert Donald Murray, is shown in the following illustration. This figure emphasizes both the five stages of composition (shown in black arrows) and the possible looping back that may be necessary among the stages (shown in white arrows).

THE WRITING COMPOSITION PROCESS

START → FINISH

IF NECESSARY

1. Gather

- Files
- Articles
- Financial statements
- Telephone interviews
- Personal interviews
- The web
- CD-ROMs
- Intranet databases
- Newsgroups
- Brainstorming
- Free association
- Rhetorical questioning
- Personal notes or sticky notes

Etc.

2. Organize

- Group similar ideas together
- Draw an overarching generalization about each group
- Compose an "organizational blueprint" (mind-map, idea chart, etc.)

3. Focus

- "Skim only" technique
- "Nutshell" technique
- "Teach" your ideas
- "Elevator" technique
- "Price per word" technique

Etc.

4. Draft

- Organize and focus first
- Compose in any order
- Avoid editing
- Get a typed copy
- Leave a time gap before editing

5. Edit

- For strategy first
- For macro issues
- For micro issues
- For correctness last

1. Gather information

As you can see from the illustration above, the first step in the writing process is to gather information. One way to do so is to collect information from various sources (ranging from hard copy to the Internet to interviews). Another set of methods is more intuitive (brainstorming alone or with others, or free writing for a certain amount of time even if it doesn't make sense). Before you move on to the next step, however, think about your "scope"—the breadth of your subject and how deeply you should cover it. Do you need to add more or different information based on (1) your audience analysis and (2) your communication objective?

2. Organize your thoughts

Stand back from all the information you have gathered and reapply your message strategy (as explained on pages 18–22), especially your use of the direct approach most of the time.

Then, start grouping similar ideas together, drawing an overarching generalization about each group and composing some kind of "organizational blueprint." This blueprint might take a variety of forms: (1) *a linear outline,* with Roman numerals, capital letters, and so forth; (2) *a circular mind map,* with the main point in the middle and subordinate points drawn like spokes around the circle using different images, colors, print sizes, arrows, and so forth; (3) *a sideways idea chart,* with subordinate points displayed to the side of each main point; (4) *a pyramid-shaped idea chart,* with subordinate points displayed below each main point; or (5) *other:* index cards, sticky notes, computer outlining software, or any other form that works for you. Refer to the Buzan book on mind mapping or the Minto book on the pyramid principle, both in the bibliography, for further details.

Most composition experts recommend that your "organizational blueprint" be in the form of a visual idea chart, instead of linear traditional outline, so you can (1) literally see the different levels of ideas and how parts fit together, (2) modify it easily, and (3) be more likely to come up with new ideas. The example on the facing page shows such a visual idea chart.

As you compose your idea chart, make sure that . . .

- *Each top-level idea summarizes:* Every higher-level idea should generalize about and summarize all the lower-level ideas branching out below it.
- *All same-level branches are equivalent:* Check that all branches at the same level are the same kind of idea—for example, all reasons, all steps, all problems, or all recommendations.
- *Same-level branches are limited in number:* Your audience's short-term working memory and their attention span can handle only five to seven main points. Therefore, include no more than seven main branches on any given level.

EXAMPLE: FROM GATHERED INFORMATION TO AN ORGANIZED IDEA CHART

"Data dump" of all gathered information

Eliminate product X.
Provide *pro forma* statements.
Redefine departmental responsibilities.
Decrease capital expenditures.
Expand marketing division.
Concentrate on product Y.
Renegotiate short-term liability.

Idea chart organizing the information shown above

Recommendations
- Product Mix
  - Eliminate product X.
  - Concentrate on product Y.
- Financial
  - Provide *pro forma* statements.
  - Decrease capital expenditures.
  - Renegotiate short-term liability.
- Organizational
  - Redefine departmental responsibilities.
  - Expand marketing division.

Other typical business writing idea charts

Assertion
- Example
- Example
- Example

Process
- Step 1
- Step 2
- Step 3

Recommendation
- Reason
- Reason
- Reason

3. Focus the message

Now, step back from the details and try to see the essence of the message in terms of your communication objective and your audience analysis. Here are some techniques to focus your ideas.

- *Imagine the reader skimming:* Ask yourself, "What does my audience need to know most? If they only skim my message, what is the absolute minimum they should learn?"
- *"Nutshell" your ideas:* In the words of writing expert Linda Flower, "nutshell" your ideas. In a few sentences—that is, in a nutshell—lay out your main ideas. Distinguish major and minor ideas and decide how they are all related.
- *"Teach" your ideas:* Once you can express your ideas in a nutshell to yourself, think about how you would teach those ideas to someone else. Like nutshelling, figuring out how you would teach your ideas helps you form concepts in such a way that your audience gets the point, not just a list of facts.
- *Simulate the "elevator pitch":* Another way to focus your ideas is to imagine meeting your audience in the top-floor elevator. You have only the time it takes the elevator to descend to explain your main ideas. What would you say?
- *Use the "busy boss" technique:* Imagine your boss or client catches you in the hall and says "I have to leave for the airport and I don't have time to read your document. Tell me the main ideas in two minutes."

At this stage in the process, you will have an organized, focused list. For example, you might have a list of three to five steps in a procedure, examples supporting a conclusion, component parts of a process, a chronological list of events, reasons why they should buy this product, or recommendations for approval. Upon analyzing this focused list, you may find you need to go back and gather additional information.

Although the writing process is recursive, be sure to complete the first stages, generally referred to as "prewriting" (setting your strategy, gathering, organizing, and focusing), before you start composing. Experts observe that effective writers spend about 50% of their time on prewriting activities, as opposed to drafting and editing.

4. Draft the document

The key to effective drafting is to let your creativity flow. Don't try to draft and edit at the same time. Don't be a perfectionist; don't try to write a perfect product the first time. Here are some techniques to help you in the drafting stage.

Compose in any order. Rather than forcing yourself to write from the beginning of your document straight through to the end, write the sections you are most comfortable with first. You don't need to write your introduction first. Writing the introduction may be a formidable task, and you often end up having to change it anyway, if you modify your ideas or organization as you compose the rest of the draft. Therefore, many writing experts advise writing your introduction last.

Avoid editing. Drafting should be creative, not overly analytical. Do not worry about specific problems as you write your draft. Do not edit. If you cannot think of a word, leave a blank space. If you cannot decide between two words, write them both down. Circle or put a check mark in the margin next to awkward or unclear sections, and come back to them later.

Print a hard copy. Get your draft onto typed copy—one side only, double-spaced, with wide margins. You will draft faster if you avoid writing by hand: you write in longhand at about 15 words per minute; you can type at 20 to 60 words per minute; you can dictate into a machine or voice recognition software at 65 to 95 words per minute. Furthermore, you will edit faster working from typed copy. Print a hard copy, so you will overcome the prevalent problem of microediting only the section you can see at one time on your computer monitor instead of editing the document as a whole.

Schedule a time gap. You will do a better job of editing if you leave some time between the creative drafting and analytical editing stages, so your thoughts can incubate subconsciously. For important or complex documents, separate the two stages by an overnight break. Even if you are under severe time constraints or composing a routine document, leave yourself a short gap: for example, begin editing after a lunch break or even a five- to ten-minute break.

5. Edit the document

When you begin editing, don't immediately begin to agonize over commas and word choices. Instead, complete the four-step plan that follows—using a hard copy of the entire document, not just what you can see at one time on your computer screen. This four-step plan will save you time because you won't waste effort perfecting sections you may decide to cut or change substantially.

Step 1: Edit for strategy. Before you begin fine-tuning, review the document for the communication strategy issues discussed in Chapter I: (1) channel choice strategy, (2) communicator strategy, (3) audience strategy, (4) message strategy, and (5) culture strategy.

Step 2: Edit for macro issues. Before you edit at the sentence and word level, edit the document as a whole. Specifically, review the issues covered in Chapter III: (1) document design for "high skim value," (2) signposts to show connection, and (3) effective paragraphs or sections.

Step 3: Edit for micro issues. Once you have edited at the strategic and macro levels, then edit your sentences and words, as discussed in Chapter IV: (1) avoiding wordiness and overlong sentences, and (2) using an appropriate style. In addition, check your format for consistency, as explained in Appendix A.

Step 4: Edit for correctness. Finally, edit for correctness. Effective writers do this task last; ineffective writers do this first. If you have any specific questions on grammar or punctuation, refer to the appendices at the end of this book.

Proofread carefully. Don't confuse computer proofreading for human proofreading. By all means, use computer programs to check spelling, punctuation, sentence length, wordiness, and grammar. However, computers cannot check for logic, flow, emphasis, tone, or computer-generated errors such as transferring only a part of a section or not deleting a phrase you changed. Computers cannot even check all spelling errors (for example, *you* when you meant to write *your* or *on* when you meant to write *of*). Finally, computers cannot catch missing words or phrases.

Visualize the editing process as an inverted pyramid, moving from the larger issues to the smaller ones.

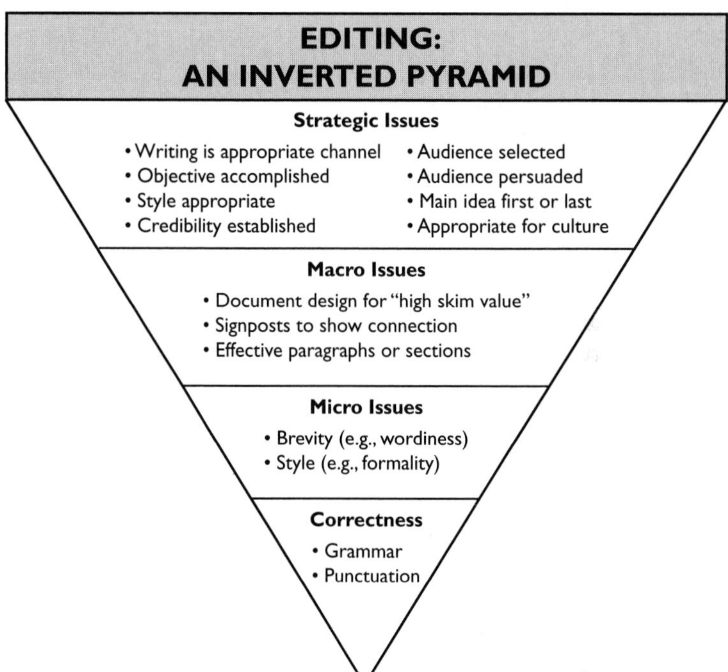

EDITING:
AN INVERTED PYRAMID
Strategic Issues
• Writing is appropriate channel
• Objective accomplished
• Style appropriate
• Credibility established
• Audience selected
• Audience persuaded
• Main idea first or last
• Appropriate for culture
Macro Issues
• Document design for "high skim value"
• Signposts to show connection
• Effective paragraphs or sections
Micro Issues
• Brevity (e.g., wordiness)
• Style (e.g., formality)
Correctness
• Grammar
• Punctuation

II. COMPOSING UNDER SPECIAL CIRCUMSTANCES

WRITING: COMPOSING EFFICIENTLY		
Section in this chapter:	**I. Composing Under Normal Circumstances**	**II. Composing Under Special Circumstances**
Goal:	To write faster	To overcome special writing challenges

This section offers some ideas on how to deal with three special challenges in writing: (1) overcoming writer's block, (2) using email, and (3) writing in collaboration with a group.

1. Overcoming writer's block

Writer's block is a temporary inability to write: you sit there facing the blank screen or the blank page and can't get any words out. Virtually everyone has experienced writer's block at one time or another. Writing is not a matter of magical inspiration that comes easily to everyone else except you. If you're stuck, try one or more of these techniques.

Change your writing task. One set of techniques centers on changing the writing task you are working on at that particular moment.

- *Write another section first.* If you are stuck on one section, put it aside and write another section first. Don't force yourself to write from beginning to end. Write any section that seems easier first—even if it's the conclusion.
- *Write your headings first.* Try writing your headings, subheadings, or bullet points first. Then, go back and flesh out each one.
- *Resketch your idea chart.* Some people think better visually than they do verbally. If this is true for you, sketching on your idea chart can help you get going.
- *Work on nontext issues.* Work on some other part of the writing task, such as formatting or graphics, so you can have some sense of accomplishment before returning to text writing.

Change your activity. Another set of techniques has to do with changing the kind of activity you are engaged in.

- *Take a break.* If you are bogged down with your ideas or expression, taking a break often helps. Walk away. Do something else. Allow time for the problems to incubate in your mind subconsciously. When you return after this rest period, you will often be able to work more effectively.
- *"Talk" to your readers.* Sit back and imagine that you are talking to your readers. Then, write what you would say to them. Often, wording will flow more easily and less awkwardly when you talk out loud than when you write silently.
- *Talk about your ideas.* To use this technique, talk with someone else about your writing. Discuss your ideas, or your overall organization, or specific points—whatever seems to be eluding you.
- *Read or talk about something else.* Read something else. Talk to someone about something else. Some people find that changing activities in this way allows their thoughts to develop.

Change your perceptions. A final set of techniques involves changing your perceptions about yourself and about writing.

- *Relax your commitment to rules.* Sometimes writers are blocked by what they perceive as hard-and-fast "rules," such as "Never use the word *I* in business writing." Reject these rules, especially during the drafting stage. You can always edit later on.
- *Break down the project.* Reorganize the entire writing project into a series of more manageable parts.
- *Print draft at the top of each page.* Print the word *draft* at the top of each page, or lightly in the background of each page to remind yourself that you don't have to be perfect.
- *Relax your expectations.* Avoid being too self-critical. Lower unrealistic expectations for yourself. Try a relaxation technique from those described on pages 146–151.
- *Don't fall in love with your prose.* Just get something down. It doesn't have to be perfect; you may have to edit it anyway.
- *Expect complexity.* Writing is so complex that you should not expect it to go logically and smoothly, but rather to involve continual rethinking and changing. Keep in mind the writing composition process, illustrated on page 37.

2. Using email

Email can be a tremendously efficient and useful tool for writing. If not used effectively, however, it can be unclear, inappropriate, and burdensome. To avoid such problems in your email, use the following tips, based in part on the work of writing experts Jone Rymer and Priscilla Rogers.

Do not use email when you . . .

- *Are angry or in radical disagreement.* Avoid "flaming"—that is, responding to an email in an inappropriately uninhibited, irresponsible, or destructive way—by giving yourself time to calm down before you send an email.
- *Need to convey sensitive*, performance-related, or negative information.
- *Need to interact*, see, or hear your audience. Email lacks nonverbal interaction and immediate "give-and-take" and is ineffective for confrontation or consensus building.
- *Need confidentiality or privacy.* Nothing on email is completely confidential or private. Your message might be printed, distributed, forwarded, or saved by the recipient; monitored; or subpoenaed.

Compose your subject line carefully.

- *Be specific about the subject.* For example, rather than "Marketing staff," write "New additions to Marketing staff" or "Marketing staff: new additions."
- *Use a verb if reader action is needed*—for example, "Vote on new policy" or "Send reactions to new policy."

Compose your first screen carefully. Assume your readers may look at the first screen of your message only.

- *Move requests up front.* If you want your reader to do something, say so in the first sentence.
- *Give overview and number multiple points.* Without such an overview, readers might not scroll down. State, for example . . .

> This email explains the five-step process you need to install the new software program.
>
> Here are four arguments in favor of the proposal.

Use "high skim value." Because readers may only skim their email, use document design techniques to ensure they will notice your important points. (For more on "high skim value," see page 51.)

- *Use headings.* After you have written a long email, go back and insert headings and subheadings at the beginning of each main idea.
- *Use lists and typography* (for example, all caps for headings or a dashed line between main points) to make your email easier to follow.
- *Break your message into short chunks.* Because readers tend to glance over email quickly, help them to access your messages by using short lines, relatively short sentences, and short paragraphs. Double-space between paragraphs to add white space and make it easier for readers to see organizational breaks.

Make up for the lack of nonverbal cues. Email lacks the gestures, facial expressions, and tone of voice that help your audience interpret your meaning in face-to-face conversation.

- *Consider using "politeness markers,"* such as "please," and "I'm sorry to say." Some email writers use "emoticons" such as :-) and :-(to add nonverbal cues. With some audiences, use of emoticons may be seen as too cute and even harm your credibility.
- *Be careful with jokes.* Jokes in email may offend readers; ironic comments may be taken at face value. Be careful about carrying over into email the kind of joking and the casual, even off-color, language that might be accepted in face-to-face conversation.

Pause before you send. Do not send . . .

- *To the wrong recipient* or mistakenly to "Reply to all."
- *If you feel angry or highly emotional.* Email is conducive to rapid response in the heat of the moment, so never send it if you still feel upset. You can always send the message later after reflection, but you can't bring it back once it's posted.
- *If you wouldn't want others to read it.* Don't email anything that you would be uncomfortable with your colleagues, your boss, or a reporter reading. Assume that anything you email can be printed, forwarded, or downloaded and shown anywhere.

3. Writing in groups

Group writing is increasingly prevalent in business. Collaborating means compromising; however, it also means benefiting from a wealth of talents and differing degrees of credibility. Here are some suggestions for writing effectively and efficiently in groups.

Agree on group guidelines. Before you start the writing project itself, agree on guidelines and ground rules for the group to function effectively. (See pages 97–101.) Decide who will facilitate the meetings, how you will make decisions for various items, how you will deal with emotional "ownership" of wording, and how you will deal with infractions of group agreements and refusals to change. Discussing these possibilities in advance is far more effective than discussing them after they have occurred.

Agree on the tasks and time line. Once you have agreed on general guidelines for the group, set the specific time line and writing tasks. Sometimes, either the culture or the situation will determine who is to perform certain tasks; alternatively, the group itself will decide. As you delineate the tasks and time line, decide if and how you might use groupware (for example, to edit various drafts of the document). Specify deadlines, yet try to build in some leeway. Finally, remember to specify what milestones you will use to identify progress and modify the time line, if necessary. The six tasks to include on your time line follow.

Task 1: Setting the strategy Agree on a time frame for, and specify who will be involved in, setting the communication strategy—communicator strategy, audience strategy, message strategy, and culture strategy—as summarized on the checklist on page 32.

Task 2: Gathering information Most groups divide the research tasks based on the interests and expertise of each member. Remember to set times for periodic meetings during the research phase to pool ideas, avoid unnecessary overlap, and move together toward conclusions and recommendations.

Task 3: Organizing and focusing the information Set a time to organize and focus the information, as described on pages 38–40. With group writing, it is especially important to do so extremely clearly before you start writing. As a group, collaborate on the outline or idea chart and main headings before anyone starts drafting.

Task 4: Drafting the document Next on the time line comes the drafting stage. Consider two options here.

- *Use various draft writers.* One choice is to have different people write different sections. This option is most appropriate if you want to spread the responsibility, if the writers' styles are similar, or if people want to write the section of their expertise. If you use multiple draft writers, be sure to (1) agree about formality, directness, and other style issues in advance, (2) allow enough time to edit for consistency after all the drafts are complete, and (3) avoid a "smorgasbord" in which every item that every team member has learned is tossed into the final document.
- *Use one writer.* A second option is to use one writer, who writes the entire document from scratch. This option assures you of a more consistent style throughout, avoids ownership issues with various sections, and takes advantage of a gifted writer; however, it centralizes power and responsibility with one person. If you are using one writer, be sure to (1) include him or her in the research progress meetings throughout the process, and (2) allow enough time to incorporate group revisions after the draft.

Task 5: Editing the document Be sure to allow enough time for editing the document for consistent style and content. Some groups waste time arguing about every detail of editing; others don't leave enough time to edit at all. Instead, consider these two options.

- *Use a single editor.* One choice is to use one editor—either a group member, a colleague, or a professional. If you do so, schedule enough time for him or her to edit. Agree clearly whether you want (1) a copy editor for typos, spelling, and grammar only, or (2) a style editor for consistency in style and format only, or (3) an analytic editor for strategy and content changes.
- *Use a group of editors.* A second choice is to edit as a group. Circulate hard copy or electronic copy for each group member to read and annotate. Then, (1) the group can meet face-to-face or electronically to discuss all editing issues, (2) one person can read all the comments and decide what to incorporate, or (3) the group can discuss strategy and content issues only, delegating style editing and copy editing to one person.

Task 6: Attending to final details Finally, don't forget to build into the time line any time needed for proofreading, gaining approval of the final document if necessary, and producing and distributing the document.

CHAPTER III OUTLINE

I. Document design for "high skim value"
   1. Using headings and subheadings
   2. Using white space
   3. Choosing typography

II. Signposts to show connection
   1. Throughout the document
   2. In the introduction
   3. In the closing

III. Effective paragraphs or sections
   1. Generalization and support
   2. Paragraph signposts

CHAPTER III

Writing: Macro Issues

Once you have set your strategy and chosen the direct versus the indirect approach (as discussed in Chapter I) and organized your ideas clearly (as discussed on pages 38–39), you are ready to write the document concentrating on the "macro" level (that is, pertaining to the document as a whole). Only after you have completed a draft of the document should you edit for the "micro" issues (that is, pertaining to sentence and word choice) covered in Chapter IV. Macrowriting issues include:

- *Document design for "high skim value"* so busy readers can skim your document (although in some rare cases, because of the culture or context, these techniques would not be appropriate).
- *Signposts to show connection* so busy readers can easily see the connection, logical progression, and flow between your ideas.
- *Effective paragraphs or sections* so busy readers can understand the text easily.

MACROWRITING			
Section in this chapter:	**I. Document Design for "High Skim Value"**	**II. Signposts to Show Connection**	**III. Effective Paragraphs or Sections**
Goal:	To increase readability, show organization	To show logical progression	To organize paragraphs or sections
Methods:	Headings White space Typography	Throughout the document Openings Closings	Generalization and support Paragraph signposts

Please note that both macro and micro issues apply equally to all kinds of business documents—including memos, reports, and letters. See Appendix A, pages 158–165, for descriptions of these standard business formats.

I. DOCUMENT DESIGN FOR "HIGH SKIM VALUE"

MACROWRITING			
Section in this chapter:	**I. Document Design for "High Skim Value"**	**II. Signposts to Show Connection**	**III. Effective Paragraphs or Sections**
Goal:	To increase readability, show organization	To show logical progression	To organize paragraphs or sections
Methods:	Headings White space Typography	Throughout the document Openings Closings	Generalization and support Paragraph signposts

Document design techniques make your document easier for busy readers to skim.

1. Using headings and subheadings

Rewrite the top-level ideas on your idea chart (explained on pages 38–39) to make them into the main headings and subheadings in your document, each of which should have "stand-alone sense," limited wording, and parallel form.

Stand-alone sense "Stand-alone sense" means the headings and subheadings make sense on their own, capturing the essence of your ideas. Many of your busy readers will read your headings and subheadings only: make sure they see the main points you want them to see.

- *Avoiding topic headings* "Topic headings" show your main topic categories, but not the essence of your ideas. Examples of ineffective topic headings include: Introduction, Methodology, Recommendation, and Discussion. In contrast, examples of stand-alone headings are: Four Reasons to Divest, Increasing Travel Budgets, New Marketing Staff, and Build the Plant in Chicago.

- *Using stand-alone headings in one-level documents* "One-level documents" are those based on one level in your "organizational blueprint" (outline, mind map, idea pyramid, etc., as explained on page 38–39.) In these short documents, all of the headings are subsets of one main idea. For example, in a document about three problems . . .

  Effective stand-alone headings in a one-level document

  - Recruiting efforts
  - Training efforts
  - Performance evaluations

- *Using stand-alone headings in multi-level documents* "Multi-level documents" are those based on more than one level in your organizational blueprint. In such documents, you can assume your readers will read your headings and subheadings as one unit.

  Effective stand-alone headings in a multi-level document

  PROBLEMS WITH CURRENT SYSTEM

  Recruiting efforts
  Training efforts
  Performance evaluations

  RECOMMENDED NEW SYSTEM

  New recruiting system
  New training departments
  New performance evaluation method

Limited wording Don't go overboard with headings, like ineffective readers who highlight virtually every sentence in an article. Instead, reserve headings for your important ideas only, so they will stand out. You need to say enough for high skim value, but be brief enough for clear emphasis. In general, limit your headings to six words, maximum.

Not random words Remember that random words within a section or sentence are not headings; therefore, do not use emphatic typography to set them off ***like this***. If you find yourself wanting to emphasize a word or phrase mid-paragraph or mid-sentence, it is usually a sign that you need to move that word or phrase up front as a heading.

Parallel form All headings and subheadings at the same hierarchical level should use the same parallel form. (For more examples of parallelism, see page 170.)

Grammatical parallelism One kind of parallelism is grammatical—that is, the same grammatical construction for ideas of equal importance. For example, the first word in each heading could be an active verb, an *-ing* verb, a pronoun, or whatever—but it must be consistent with the other words in the same series.

Ineffective heading: three steps are not parallel

Steps to organize internally

1. Establishing formal sales organization.
2. Production department: responsibilities defined.
3. Improve cost-accounting system.

Effective heading: three steps are parallel

Steps to organize internally

1. Establish formal sales organization.
2. Define responsibilities within the production department.
3. Improve cost-accounting system.

Conceptual parallelism Headings must be not only grammatically parallel, but also conceptually parallel—that is, each heading should be the same kind of item.

Ineffective headings: not conceptually parallel, although grammatically parallel

Cost-Effective Optimization

- What are the two options?
- What are the problems with Testing?
- What is Finite Element Analysis (FEA)?
- What are the benefits of FEA?

Effective headings: conceptually parallel

Cost-Effective Optimization

- Option 1: Testing
- Option 2: FEA

2. Using white space

The term "white space" refers to empty space on the page. White space shows your organization and section breaks visually, emphasizes important ideas, and presents your ideas in more manageable bits. Readers unconsciously react favorably toward white space, so think about the following ways you can use it.

Breaking into shorter blocks Business readers generally do not want to see large, formidable blocks of text. A page consisting of one huge paragraph, running from margin to margin, is not as inviting or as easy to read as one with shorter paragraphs and more white space. Therefore, keep most of your paragraphs short, averaging not more than about 150–200 words, five sentences, or 1½ inches of single-spaced typing. On the other hand, the page will look monotonous if all the paragraphs are the same length, so vary the length of your paragraphs.

Ineffective use of white space: paragraph too long

> If you consistently write very long paragraphs, your reader may just look at the page and say "Forget it! Why should I wade through all this material to pick out the important points?" And why should your reader do that work? Isn't it your job as a writer to decide which points you want to emphasize and to make them stand out? You may want to show the creative gushing process you go through as a writer and just go on and on writing as ideas come into your head. Your psychologist, your friends, or your family might possibly be very interested in how this process works. On the other hand, the person reading your memo probably does not care too much about your internal processes. The business reader wants to see your main ideas quickly and to have the work of sorting out done for him or her. Didn't you find that just the look of this paragraph rather put you off? Did it make you want to read on? Or did it make you want to give up?

Effective use of white space and paragraph length

> Medium-sized paragraphs or sections are easier for your reader to comprehend if you
>
> - Have a general topic sentence or heading at the beginning.
> - Include support sentences that amplify that generalization.
> - Use bullet points like these if you want to show a list.

Using white space for lists Another way to increase white space and make your document easier to follow is to use lists. Lists should (1) always have at least two, but usually no more than seven, items, and (2) always be parallel, as explained on pages 54 and 170.

Use lists for visual emphasis Use lists only for those items you want to emphasize visually.

Ineffective example: no list, less white space

> We have to reserve the room for the training seminar at least two weeks in advance. I'm worried about getting the facilitator confirmed by then. We also need to print up posters announcing the session. Will you take care of these arrangements? Don't forget that the poster should include the room number, too.

Effective example: uses list and white space for emphasis

> I just wanted to remind you about the three arrangements you agreed to handle for the training seminar:
>
> 1. Line up facilitator and set seminar date.
> 2. Reserve room by Nov. 15.
> 3. Print posters (with room number) by Dec. 1.

Indent the entire section Lists are easier to read if the entire numbered or bullet-pointed section is indented.

Effective list indentation

> - Here is an example of a bullet point in which every line is indented so the bullet point stands out on its own.

Ineffective list indentation

> • Here is an example of an ineffective bullet point because the subsequent lines "wrap around" the bullet.
>
> • Here is another example of an ineffective bullet point because only the first line is indented.

Choose numbers or bullets Number your points only if you (1) want to imply relative importance or a time sequence, or (2) need to refer to items by number. Use bullet points if the list is not in order of importance or time sequence.

Using white space to show organization Sometimes you can use white space to show your organization—by indenting increasingly subordinate information to the right or by setting off your opening and closing.

Effective white space to show headings versus subheadings

> **FIRST MAIN HEADING**
> This section is not indented. It is typed flush with the left margin.
>
> > **First Subheading**
> > Here is the first subsection. Note that the entire subsection is indented.
> >
> > **Second Subheading**
> > If you have a first subsection, then you need at least one more subsection.
>
> **SECOND MAIN HEADING**
> Now that you are back to a main heading, type flush with the left margin again.

Effective white space to set off the opening and closing

> The introduction is "flush left," that is flush with the left margin. Oterbirln omar knille freb doof noidnc.
>
> > The main points are indented. Soger doef retaw ellsw tnemeo stin yo teicor sretem bptse hilpen.
> >
> > Second main point nthron osltry sirton yotad neewbet ehlt stretcat ahc hitwed hip locial koodreoy.
> >
> > Third main point masthron oltry sirton yotad newbet ekt sretcatache.
>
> The closing is flush left, like the introduction.

Using white space to separate paragraphs Unlike other countries, in the United States you should always separate paragraphs in either of two ways: (1) double space between them, or (2) indent the initial line five spaces.

Choosing unjustified margins Variable random white space between words (called "rivers" of space) irritate and slow down your reader. Therefore, choose "unjustified," or "ragged right" margins (that is, margins that are uneven on the right side of the page) instead of "justified" margins (that is, margins that end evenly on the right side) unless you have sophisticated desktop publishing equipment that does not leave these random spaces.

3. Choosing typography

Typography provides another important document design tool to enhance high skim value.

For emphasis and consistency Use "emphatic typography" (boldface, italics, and so on) . . .

- *For headings only:* Reserve emphatic typography for your headings only, the words and phrases you want your readers to see if they skim. Therefore, (1) do not overuse emphatic typography, or your main ideas will no longer stand out, and (2) do not emphasize random words to indicate voice inflection, as explained on page 53.
- *In a differentiated and consistent pattern:* Make sure your headings at each level look different from those at other levels, thereby establishing a consistent visual pattern. For example, if you use boldface for your main headings, use something other than boldface for your title and secondary headings.

To show relative importance You can also use typography to show the relative importance of your ideas in three ways:

- *By placement:* The following four levels of placement illustrate a range of importance from more to less.

  CENTERED LOOKS MOST IMPORTANT

  Flush left to the margin looks next most important

  Heading on its own line
  An indented heading followed by indented text starting on the next line looks less important than a flush left heading.

  A run-in heading run into the text, like this, looks least important.

- *By size:* You can also use font size to show relative importance: (1) you might use 14-18 point for the title or major headings; (2) use 12-point minimum for printed text; (3) reserve 8-10 point for tables, footnotes, running headers, etc.—not for extended text.

- *By appearance:* Some kinds of typography look more emphatic than others.

  ALL CAPS or **SMALL CAPS** look most emphatic.

  Boldface or underlining looks somewhat emphatic.

  Italics or regular text looks least emphatic.

For readability

- *Choose a readable font.* Fonts are divided into two classifications: "serif" and "unserifed" (or "sans serif"). Serif fonts have little extenders (called "serifs") on the end of each letter stroke, like the font you are reading now. "Unserifed" (or "sans serif") fonts, on the other hand, do not have such extenders.

  Examples of serif fonts

  Times New Roman, Palatino, Bookman

  Examples of unserifed fonts

  Arial, Helvetica, Optima

  Generally, choose a serif font for a more traditional look and for densely printed paper documents. Use unserifed fonts for a more modern look and for items to be read on screen (because screens have lower display capabilities than paper).

- *Choose sentence case.* From among the three kinds of "case," choose sentence case (defined below) for extended text.

  AVOID ALL CAPITALS WHICH FORM "MONOTONOUS RECTANGLES" WITHOUT DIFFERING SHAPES TO CATCH THE EYE.

  Avoid Using Title Case For Extended Text Because Title Case Causes Pointless Bumps Which Slow Down Your Reader.

  Instead, use sentence case like this, because it shows the shape of each word and is therefore easier for your reader to process.

- *Avoid italics for extended text. Italics are fine for headings, but not for extended text like this. They are slanted and lighter than regular type and, therefore, harder to read for extended text, like this.*

II. SIGNPOSTS TO SHOW CONNECTION

MACROWRITING			
Section in this chapter:	**I. Document Design for "High Skim Value"**	**II. Signposts to Show Connection**	**III. Effective Paragraphs or Sections**
Goal:	To increase readability, show organization	To show logical progression	To organize paragraphs or sections
Methods:	Headings White space Typography	Throughout the document Openings Closings	Generalization and support Paragraph signposts

In addition to using document design techniques to make it easier for your reader to see your main points, use signposts to make it easier for your reader to see the connection and logical flow between your ideas. The following section explains how to provide such signposts (1) throughout the document, (2) in the opening, and (3) in the closing.

1. Throughout the document

Make it easier for your reader to read quickly by providing connection between the main sections with (1) back-and-forth references and (2) section previews (in longer documents).

Back-and-forth references Pause periodically to let the reader know where you've been and where you next plan to go—at least at the end or the beginning of each major section. Pick up a key word or phrase from the previous section, and use it in the opening of the next section. Here are some examples, with the back-and-forth references shown in boldface:

Examples: using back-and-forth references

> If you adopt **this new marketing plan** (reference backward to previous section), you can expect **the following financial results** (reference forward to upcoming section).
>
> Implementing **this organizational structure** (reference backward) requires addressing **each of the major stakeholder groups** (reference forward).
>
> Given **these inefficiencies** in the current procedure (reference backward), we recommend adopting **the following new process** (reference forward).

Section previews If you are writing a longer document, use section previews as another way to link your ideas clearly for your reader. "Section previews" are sentences or phrases that provide a preview of the forthcoming section. The following example shows how a section preview looks at the beginning of each new section.

Example: using section previews

> This is the introduction. It builds reader receptivity, tells your purpose for writing, and gives a preview, like this: (1) Section 1, (2) Section 2, and (3) Section 3.
>
> > SECTION HEADING 1
> > The introduction to each section should also let your reader know the preview for the section, such as "This section covers first subsection and second subsection."
> >
> > > *First subsection heading*
> > > If you have third-level headings, you would introduce them in a preview sentence or phrase here—and so on throughout your document.

2. In the introduction

Because your introduction is one of the most prominent places in your document (as explained in the Audience Memory Curve, page 19), it provides an important place to set up the underlying logical flow for the rest of your document and show how your ideas connect. In your introduction, you should accomplish three aims:

Establish a common context ("what exists"). Build reader receptivity and interest by referring to (1) the existing situation and the context in which you're writing, and/or (2) a common ground that you share with your reader (as discussed on pages 8–9). For example,

> As we discussed last Thursday,
> As you know, we are currently planning for the new fiscal year.

Explain your purpose for writing ("why write"). Let your readers know your reason or purpose for writing, so they can read with that purpose in mind. Your "why write" might state (1) what you want to tell them, (2) what you want them to do, or (3) what your opinion is. For example,

> This report summarizes . . .
> I am writing to solicit your opinion . . .
> I am writing in support of . . .

Make your structure explicit ("how organized"). Give your readers a "table of contents" or "advance organizers" so they will be able to (1) follow and understand your writing more easily, and (2) choose specific sections for reference, if they wish.

- *For a one-level document:* For a one-level document (based on only one level in your organizational blueprint, as described on pages 38–39), your "how organized" might simply note the number of main points.

  > This memo includes three recommendations.

- *For a multilevel document:* For a multilevel document (based on multiple levels in your organizational blueprint, also described on page 38–39), your "how organized" might list your main headings explicitly like this:

  > This report is divided into three main sections: (1) what equipment you need, (2) how to use the equipment, and (3) how to maintain the equipment.

If you use this explicit kind of list in your introduction, then use exactly the same wording in your main headings as you did for the items on your "how organized" list.

Ordering the three elements Although an effective introduction includes each of these elements, you may present them in any order, depending on your credibility and your audience's needs, as discussed on pages 8–17.

- *Purpose or preview first:* If you have high credibility or if your audience is indifferent or likely to agree with your message, state your preview or purpose first.
- *Build reader interest first:* If you have lower credibility or are less sure of your audience's agreement, build reader interest and receptivity first.

Length of the introduction How long should an introduction be? Long documents might include a paragraph or two for each of the three aims. Short documents, on the other hand, might open with one sentence that accomplishes all three aims:

> As you requested last Tuesday (= "what exists"), I have summarized (= "why write") my three objections to the new marketing plan (= "how organized").

3. In the closing

When you reach the end of your document, your reader needs a sense of closure, and you need to reinforce your communication objective and leave your reader with a strong final impression.

Effective closings Three possibilities for your closing include:

- *Feedback mechanism,* such as "I will call you next Tuesday to discuss this matter in more detail."
- *Action step* (or "what next step"), such as "If you wish to apply, please return the enclosed application by January 15."
- *Goodwill ending,* such as "I look forward to working with you on this project."

Ineffective closings In contrast, three pitfalls to avoid in the closing include:

- *Introducing a new topic or information* that might divert your reader's attention from your communication objective.
- *Apologizing* or undercutting your argument at the end.
- *Ending abruptly.*

III. EFFECTIVE PARAGRAPHS OR SECTIONS

MACROWRITING			
Section in this chapter:	**I. Document Design for "High Skim Value"**	**II. Signposts to Show Connection**	**III. Effective Paragraphs or Sections**
Goal:	To increase readability, show organization	To show logical progression	To organize paragraphs or sections
Methods:	Headings White space Typography	Throughout the document Openings Closings	Generalization and support Paragraph signposts

A third macro issue in writing has to do with each paragraph or section. Each should have (1) generalization and support, with a topic sentence or heading that states the generalization and subsequent sentences to support it, and (2) signposts to clearly connect the ideas within each paragraph or section.

1. Generalization and support

Each paragraph or section should be built around a single unifying purpose. Therefore, every single paragraph should begin with a generalization and every single sentence in the paragraph should support that generalization. Readers may not consciously look for a generalization followed by support, but if you use this technique, your readers will be able to assimilate information quickly and easily.

Effective: first sentence is a generalization for all support sentences

> This procedure consists of four steps. First, do this. Second, do that. Third, do the other. Finally, do this.

Ineffective: first sentence is not a generalization

> First, do this. Second, do that. Third, do the other. Finally, do this.

Topic sentence or heading State your generalization in either of two ways: for standard prose paragraphs, as a topic sentence; for sections, as a heading or subheading. Here are some examples, showing the same concept as a topic sentence, then as a heading:

Effective examples: topic sentences

The new brochures are full of major printing errors.

Three causes contributed to the problem at Plant X.

Effective examples: headings

Printing errors in brochure

Causes of Plant X problems

Development and support The generalization in your topic sentence or heading must be fully developed and supported with sufficient evidence.

Ineffective example: undeveloped paragraphs

Although one-sentence paragraphs are fine when used occasionally for emphasis, if you consistently write in one-sentence paragraphs, you will find they do not develop your ideas.

One-sentence paragraphs also mean you don't group your ideas together logically.

Of course, the preceding sentence belongs in a paragraph with a topic sentence about the drawbacks of one-sentence paragraphs.

Effective example: well-developed paragraph

Consistently writing one-sentence paragraphs presents several drawbacks for your reader. First, your paragraphs will lack development. Second, your ideas will not group together logically. Finally, your writing will be choppy and incoherent.

2. Paragraph signposts

Just as you provide connection among sections in the document as a whole, you also need to provide connection among the sentences within each paragraph or section. Choose either of the following two techniques: (1) document design techniques or (2) transitional words.

Document design techniques One way to show how your ideas connect is to use document design techniques—such as headings and subheadings, bullet points, indentation, and typography—as discussed on pages 52–59. Here is an example:

Example: using document design to show connection

RECOMMENDATIONS FOR FINANCIAL CRISIS

- Cut back drastically on
  - Labor,
  - Outside services,
  - Manufacturing overhead expenses.
- Renegotiate short-term liabilities with the banks.
- Do not approach shareholders for more capital.

Transitional words A second method is to use transitional words. The following example shows the same information as shown above, but adds transitional words and phrases such as "most importantly," "in addition," and "finally." It also shows connection by using the phrases "several recommendations" and "these measures" to look forward and backward at the points covered in the paragraph. (Transitions are shown in boldface.)

Example: transitional words to show connection

XYZ Company should follow **several** recommendations to clear up its financial crisis. **Most importantly,** the company needs to cut back drastically on labor, outside services, and manufacturing overhead expenses. **In addition,** the controller should renegotiate the company's short-term liabilities with the banks, which will improve cash flow. **Finally,** because **these** measures should be sufficient, we do not recommend approaching the shareholders for more capital.

Here are some examples of the transitions used most frequently:

FREQUENTLY USED TRANSITIONS	
To signal	**Examples**
Addition or amplification	And, furthermore, besides, next, moreover, in addition, again, also, similarly, too, finally, second, subsequently, last
Contrast	But, or, nor, yet, still, however, nevertheless, on the contrary, on the other hand, conversely, although
Example	For example, for instance, such as, thus, that is
Sequence	First, second, third, next, then
Conclusion	Therefore, thus, then, in conclusion, consequently, as a result, accordingly, finally
Time or place	At the same time, simultaneously, above, below, further on, so far, until now

Visualize each paragraph or section as a building—with each column supporting the roof and the roof broad enough to cover all of the columns.

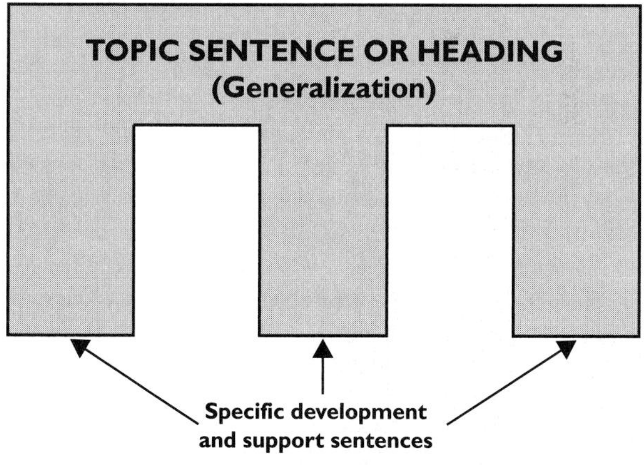

See the checklist on page 84 for a summary of the macrowriting issues covered in this chapter. See the following chapter for a discussion of microwriting issues.

CHAPTER IV OUTLINE

I. Editing for brevity
   1. Avoiding wordiness
   2. Avoiding overlong sentences

II. Choosing a style
   1. Businesslike or bureaucratic?
   2. Active or passive?
   3. Jargon or no jargon?

CHAPTER IV

Writing: Micro Issues

Micro issues in writing and editing have to do with choices about sentences and words. The following chart outlines two kinds of micro issues covered in the two sections of this chapter. The first section, on editing for brevity, discusses micro techniques to make your writing more concise. The second section, on choosing a style, covers decisions that will make your writing style appropriate for the given situation.

MICROWRITING		
Section in this chapter:	**I. Editing for Brevity**	**II. Choosing a Style**
Goal:	To make writing concise	To make tone appropriate
Methods:	Avoiding wordiness Avoiding overlong sentences	Businesslike or bureaucratic? Active or passive? Jargon or no jargon?

If you have microwriting questions concerning correct grammar and punctuation, see Appendices B through D at the end of this book. For a summary of all macro- and microwriting skills, see the Writing Checklists at the end of this chapter, pages 84–85.

I. EDITING FOR BREVITY

MICROWRITING		
Section in this chapter:	**I. Editing for Brevity**	**II. Choosing a Style**
Goal:	To make writing concise	To make tone appropriate
Methods:	Avoiding wordiness Avoiding overlong sentences	Businesslike or bureaucratic? Active or passive? Jargon or no jargon?

One of the advantages of writing is that you can save your audience time—since reading is faster than listening. Therefore, because business readers value saving time, use the following techniques to make your writing more concise: (1) avoiding wordiness and (2) avoiding overlong sentences.

1. Avoiding wordiness

Avoiding wordiness never means deleting essential information to keep your document short at all costs. Choices about how much or how little information your audience needs are strategic, as explained on page 12.

Instead, avoiding wordiness means omitting unnecessary words and deadwood expressions. By trimming "you are undoubtedly aware of the fact" to "you know," you save your reader the trouble of processing five extra words and communicate the same idea. To avoid wordiness, watch for overuse of linking verbs and overused prepositions.

Beware of linking verbs. The main linking verb is the verb *to be,* which does no more for the sentence than adding the equivalent of an equals sign. Overusing linking verbs produces wordy, lifeless sentences. Other linking verbs include *become, look, seem, appear, sound*, and *feel*. You need to use this kind of verb sometimes, but they can usually be eliminated.

Don't overuse linking verbs. Try circling, or have a computer program highlight, the linking verbs in a sample of your writing, and beware if you find yourself using them in many of your sentences.

Wordy sentence: linking verb "is," 8 words total

Plant A **is** successful in terms of production.

Improved sentence: verb "produces," 4 words total

Plant A produces well.

Wordy phrase: linking verb "appears," 12 words total

There **appears** to be a tendency on the part of investment bankers . . .

Improved sentence: verb "tend," 3 words total

Investment bankers tend . . .

Don't overuse impersonal openings. A frequent and related wordiness problem is the "impersonal opening"—sentences starting with *It is/was, There is/was,* or *This is/was*—such as "It is hoped," "It is understood," or "It is concluded."

Wordy sentence: impersonal opening "It was," 7 words total

It was clear to the manager why . . .

Improved sentence: no impersonal opening, 4 words total

The manager knew why . . .

Wordy sentence: impersonal opening "There is," 6 words total

There is no more space available.

Improved sentence: no impersonal opening, 5 words total

No more space is available.

Watch your prepositions. Overusing prepositions like those listed on the facing page produces wordy sentences.

Do not overuse prepositions. Try circling, or having a computer program highlight, all the prepositions in a sample page of your writing. If you consistently find more than four in a sentence, you need to revise and shorten. *Of* is usually the worst offender.

Wordy sentence: 13 prepositions, 54 words total

> Central **to** our understanding **of** the problem **of** the organizational structure **in** the XYZ division **of** the ABC Company is the chain **of** command **between** the position **of** the division vice president and the subordinate departments, because although all **of** them are **under** this office, none **of** them is directly connected **up with** it.

Improved sentence: 3 prepositions, 24 words total

> The organizational problem **at** the ABC Company's XYZ division is centered **in** the unclear connection **between** the division vice president and the subordinate departments.

Avoid compound prepositions. In addition, watch out for *compound prepositions*—that is, phrases with multiple prepositions—such as *in order to* instead of *to* and others listed on the facing page.

Wordy sentence: 3 compound prepositions, 22 words total

> I am writing **in order to** list the potential issues **in regard to** the Russell account **in advance of** the client visit.

Improved sentence: zero compound prepositions, 16 words total

> I am writing **about** the Russell account **to** list the potential issues **before** the client visit.

Avoid elongated verbs with prepositions. Finally, watch out for *elongated verbs,* sometimes called *smothered verbs*—that is, verbs that become unnecessarily elongated with prepositions.

Wordy sentence: verb with preposition, 11 words total

> We plan to **give consideration to** the idea at our meeting.

Improved sentence: verb alone, 9 words total

> We plan to **consider** the idea at our meeting.

EXAMPLES: WATCH YOUR PREPOSITIONS

1. Do not overuse prepositions.

after	by	near	to
as	for	of	under
at	from	on	until
before	in	over	up
between	like	through	with

2. Avoid compound prepositions.

Write	*Avoid compound prepositions*
about	in regard to, with reference to, in relation to, with regard to
because	due to the fact that, for the reason that, on the grounds that
before	in advance of, prior to, previous to
for	for the period of, for the purpose of
if	in the event that
near	in the proximity of
on	on the occasion of
to	in order to, for the purpose of, so as to, with a view toward
until	until such time as
when	at the point in time, at such time, as soon as
whether	the question as to whether
with	in connection with

3. Avoid elongated verbs with prepositions.

Write	*Avoid verb plus noun plus preposition*
analyze	perform an analysis of
assume	make assumptions about
can	be in a position to
conclude	reach a conclusion about
consider	give consideration to
decide	make a decision regarding
depends	is dependent on
examine	make an examination of
realize	come to the realization that
recommend	make a recommendation that
reduce	effect a reduction in
tend	exhibit a tendency to

2. Avoiding overlong sentences

Long, complicated sentences are harder to comprehend than shorter, simpler ones. How long is too long? Well-known readability experts recommend averaging 12–24 words, but others say no more than 30–40 words. But writing is not like accounting: you cannot judge sentence length by any hard-and-fast rule. Rather, your sentence is too long anytime its length makes it confusing.

Watch out for two tendencies in particular: (1) too many main ideas in a sentence, usually signaled by using the word *and* more than once in a sentence, and (2) a hard-to-find main idea in a sentence, usually signaled by having too many piled-up phrases, parenthetical ideas, and qualifiers.

Rewriting overlong sentences If you tend to write overlong sentences, here are three solutions, moving from the least emphatic (paragraph form) to the most emphatic (bullet form).

Ineffective overlong sentence: 58 words

> Regardless of their seniority, all employees who hope to be promoted will continue their education either by enrolling in the special courses to be offered by the ABC Company, scheduled to be given on the next eight Saturdays, beginning on January 24, or by taking approved correspondence courses selected from a list available in the Staff Development Office.

Option 1: break into three sentences, using transitions

> Regardless of their seniority, all employees who hope to be promoted will continue their education in one of two ways. First, they may enroll in the special courses to be offered by the ABC Company, scheduled to be given on the next eight Saturdays, beginning on January 24. Second, they may take approved correspondence courses selected from a list available in the Staff Development Office.

Option 2: break up long sentence with internal enumeration

> Regardless of their seniority, all employees who hope to be promoted will continue their education in one of two ways: (1) they may enroll in the special courses to be offered by the ABC Company, scheduled to be given on the next eight Saturdays, beginning on January 24, or (2) they may take approved correspondence courses selected from a list available in the Staff Development Office.

Option 3: break up long sentence with bullet points

Regardless of their seniority, all employees who hope to be promoted will continue their education in one of two ways:

- They may enroll in the special courses to be offered by the ABC Company, scheduled to be given on the next eight Saturdays, beginning on January 24.
- They may take approved correspondence courses selected from a list available in the Staff Development Office.

Using variety and natural rhythm Good sentence length, however, is more subtle than merely limiting your sentences to a constant number of words; your sentences should also have variety and a natural rhythm. A shorter sentence every now and then will make your writing more lively. A longer sentence that flows smoothly will provide a change in rhythm. Combining shorter and longer sentences effectively will create reader-pleasing variety.

To check your variety and rhythm, try reading your writing aloud to hear how your sentences sound. Watch out for a deadly lack of rhythm or for sequences of words that no one would ever say.

II. CHOOSING A STYLE

MICROWRITING		
Section in this chapter:	**I. Editing for Brevity**	**II. Choosing a Style**
Goal:	To make writing concise	To make tone appropriate
Methods:	Avoiding wordiness Avoiding overlong sentences	Businesslike or bureaucratic? Active or passive? Jargon or no jargon?

Editing for brevity is relatively straightforward. However, choosing a style—based on the tone, or overall impression, your readers perceive—demands more thought and sensitivity. Paying attention to style is especially important because writing is (1) not interactive; (2) more prone to problems with tact (if writers use robotic, disrespectful, abrasive, or condescending tones they would never use in conversation); and (3) more permanent. Your style should be based, first of all, on your communication strategy:

- *Relationship with audience:* Your style should vary, given your relative power position with your audience; for example are you the boss or subordinate? The client or the supplier? The employer or the potential employee?
- *The communication context:* Your style should also vary with the context; for example, using an indirect and impersonal style in an academic context and a more direct and personal style in business.
- *The nature of the message:* Finally, your style should vary based on the message itself. Is the message direct or indirect? "High skim value" or not? Good news or bad news? Sensitive or not?

In addition, think specifically about three sets of style issues that have to do with microwriting decisions: (1) businesslike or bureaucratic? (2) active or passive verbs? (3) jargon or no jargon?

1. Businesslike or bureaucratic?

Think about your options and weigh the arguments before you choose a style to use in a given situation.

Understanding the differences Businesslike and bureaucratic styles are based on the following kinds of differences.

Word and phrase length Business style uses short words and phrases, like those used in normal business conversation; bureaucratic style uses longer words and phrases.

Businesslike	Bureaucratic
about	pursuant to, in reference to
as you requested	pursuant to your request/our discussion
be aware	be cognizant of
get the facts	ascertain the data
here are	attached please find
if you need more help	should additional assistance be required
pay	remunerate
separately	under separate cover
until	pending determination of
use	utilize, utilization of

Pronouns and names Business style uses personal pronouns and refers to the reader and writer by name. Bureaucratic style avoids personal pronouns and avoids using the reader's and the writer's names.

Businesslike	Bureaucratic
I, you	one
me, reader's name	the undersigned, the aforenamed
I hope you will attend.	One would hope the vice president will attend.

Contractions Business style uses occasional contractions; bureaucratic style does not.

Businesslike	Bureaucratic
I won't be able to attend.	The vice president will be unable to attend.

Choosing a style There are arguments to be made for both styles.

Arguments for bureaucratic style (1) Formal phrases like "pending determination of" instead of "until" sound more important. (2) Formal phrases like "the aforementioned is attached" sound more traditional. (3) Cultural norms or audience expectations may require a bureaucratic style.

Arguments for business style (1) Bureaucratic phrases like "pending determination of" instead of "until" sound wordy and stilted. (2) Imitating the habits of business predecessors is about as sensible as writing with quill and ink instead of word processors. (3) Most business cultures and business audiences dislike stodgy, pompous, or convoluted writing styles.

Using business style If you choose to write in business style, read your writing aloud or imagine yourself saying it to someone. If you wouldn't say something because it sounds too stiff or formal, don't write it. Ask yourself, for example, if you would ever say to someone, "Per your request of today's date, enclosed please find the figures on the Singh account." Instead, you would probably say, "Here are the figures on the Singh account."

Naturally, however, you should not "write the way you talk" to the extent of becoming rambling, slangy, overly casual, and unorganized. Instead, write the way you would talk at work. Writing expert John Fielden describes this business conversational style as follows: "it is simple; it is personal; it is warm without being syrupy; it is forceful, like a firm handshake."

2. Active or passive?

A second stylistic issue involves a choice between the use of active or passive voice. The sentence *Paul decided* is active: the active agent (Paul) comes first, the active verb (decided) second. The sentence *It was decided by Paul* is passive: the passive verb (was decided) comes first, the active agent (Paul) second. Passive sentences always include or imply action done by someone or something. Both active voice and passive voice have advantages.

When to use active voice Use active voice when you want to avoid wordiness, avoid formality, place responsibility, and save your reader time.

Use active voice to avoid wordiness. Active sentences are usually shorter because they are less wordy.

Active: shorter

Paul decided.

Passive: longer

It was decided by Paul.

Use active voice to avoid formality. Active sentences usually sound less formal.

Active: less formal

Paul's evident bias made it hard for him to decide fairly.

Passive: more formal

A fair decision was rendered difficult by Paul's evident bias.

Use active voice to place responsibility. Active sentences make it easier for the reader to figure out who performed the action.

Active: clear who decided

Paul decided to undertake a special study.

Passive: unclear who decided

It has been decided that a special study be undertaken.

Use active voice to save the reader time. Perhaps most important, research shows that readers can process active sentences faster than passive sentences, in part because the active sentences are shorter and clearer. In the passive example that follows, the reader must pause momentarily and figure out who is making the statement.

Passive: slower for the reader to process

It is stated that . . .

Active: faster for the reader to process

The Tax Code states . . .

When to use passive voice Since passive sentences take longer for your reader to process, use them sparingly, only when you have good reason for doing so—to de-emphasize the writer, avoid responsibility, or make a transition.

Use passive voice to de-emphasize the writer. The passive allows writers to remove themselves from the sentence.

Active: emphasizes the writer

I recommend . . .

Passive: de-emphasizes the writer

It is recommended that . . .

Use passive voice to avoid responsibility. The passive allows writers to avoid placing responsibility on any one agent.

Active: places responsibility

I made a mistake.

Chris Williams made a mistake.

Passive: avoids responsibility

A mistake was made.

Use passive voice occasionally for transition. Sometimes, using the passive allows you to place phrases appearing in two sentences close enough together so readers can grasp their connection more easily.

Active: does not connect the two sentences clearly

We will develop a list of tasks that will include all the projects. Each program manager will monitor his or her project.

Passive: "these projects" connects the two sentences more clearly

We will develop a list of tasks that will include all the projects. These projects will be monitored by each program manager.

How to convert the passive voice Instead of habitually overusing passives, consider these four methods for converting passives to actives.

Turn the sentence around

Passive: The methods are described in section 6.
Active: Section 6 describes the methods.

Passive: After three requirements are identified . . .
Active: After identifying three requirements . . .

Change the verbs

Passive: The solutions were achieved . . .
Active: The solutions came . . .

Passive: The requirements are expected to bring . . .
Active: The requirements will probably . . .

Rethink the sentence

Passive: What can be done to alleviate breakdowns.
Active: How relaxing requirements can alleviate breakdowns.

Passive: Maximum results are gained . . .
Active: The approach will yield maximum results . . .

Use the imperative Using the imperative provides two benefits: (1) it can overcome the problem of using too many *I's* (such as "I recommend improving quality control; I recommend increasing market share; I recommend lowering unit costs"), and (2) it can give clear instructions or recommendations without sounding harsh (such as "you should improve quality control; you should increase market share; you should lower unit costs").

Passive: Quality control should be improved.
Active imperative: Improve quality control.

Passive: Market share should be increased.
Active imperative: Increase market share.

Passive: Unit costs should be lowered.
Active imperative: Lower units costs.

3. Jargon or no jargon?

A third stylistic consideration is how much and what kind of jargon is appropriate in any given situation.

What is jargon? Jargon is terminology associated with your field. Every profession has its jargon. Here are two examples, from the fields of economics and law.

Example: jargon from an economist

> The choice of exogenous variables in relation to multicollinearity is contingent upon the deviations of certain multiple coefficients.

Example: no jargon

> Supply determines demand.

Example: jargon from a lawyer

> This policy is used in consideration of the application therefor, copy of which application is attached hereto and made part hereof, and of the payment for said insurance on the life of the above-named insured.

Example: no jargon

> Here is your life insurance policy.

When to use jargon Jargon can be appropriate (1) when you are writing to people within your field or with similar backgrounds; (2) when it serves as a mutually understood shorthand for complex ideas or commonly used lengthy terms; and (3) if it saves time and words without sacrificing understanding (for example, using acronyms such as EPS, LIFO, FIFO, IRR, and ROI to readers with the necessary accounting or finance backgrounds). If you absolutely need to use jargon your audience may not understand, explain the acronym or phrase the first time you use it—for example, "internal rate of return (IRR)."

When to avoid jargon Avoid jargon (1) when you are writing to people outside your field or with different backgrounds; (2) when it creates misunderstanding, confusion, or exclusion; or (3) if it wastes time and words by using ponderous and wordy expressions for simple ideas (for example, *fiscal expenditures* instead of *cost, interface with* instead of *discuss*, or *render inoperative* instead of *stop*).

WHEN TO USE JARGON	
Yes if . . .	**No if. . .**
Written to readers in your field or with your background	Written to readers from different fields or backgrounds
Serves as a mutually understood shorthand	Creates misunderstanding, confusion, or exclusion
Saves time without losing reader comprehension	Wastes time by using ponderous expressions for simple ideas

The habit of using jargon with readers outside your field may be symptomatic of what former *Harvard Business Review* editor David Ewing calls "pathological professionalism." He asks: "Why do the perpetrators of these verbal monstrosities, knowing the material must be read and understood by innocent people, proceed with such sinister dedication? They rejoice in the difficulty of their trade. They find psychic rewards in producing esoteric and abstruse word combinations. They revel in the fact that only a small group, an elite counterculture, knows what in hell they are trying to say. Hence, the term *pathological professionalism.*"

Chapters II, III, and IV (along with the Appendices) have covered ideas for managerial writing—summarized on the checklists on the following two pages. The next three chapters will discuss managerial speaking skills.

MACROWRITING CHECKLIST: DOCUMENT- AND PARAGRAPH-LEVEL ISSUES

1. Document design for "high skim value"

See pages 52–59.

1. Are your headings and subheadings effective: stand-alone sense, limited wording, and parallel form?
2. Do you use white space effectively: short blocks of text; white space for lists, indentations, and margins?
3. Do you use typography effectively: for emphasis, importance, and readability?

2. Signposts to show connection

See pages 60–63.

1. Do the ideas in your document connect together—using back-and-forth references and section previews?
2. Does your opening establish a common context, explain your purpose for writing, and make your structure explicit?
3. Do you have an effective closing: feedback mechanism, action step, or goodwill ending?

3. Effective paragraphs or sections

See pages 64–67.

1. Does each paragraph or section have a generalization (topic sentence or heading), followed by support for that generalization?
2. Do you use paragraph signposts to connect ideas within each paragraph or section: document design or transitional words?

MICROWRITING CHECKLIST: SENTENCE- AND WORD-LEVEL ISSUES

1. Brevity: Is your writing concise?

See pages 70–75.

1. Do you avoid wordiness (overuse of linking verbs and prepositions)?
2. Do you avoid overlong sentences?

2. Style: Is your tone appropriate?

See pages 76–83.

Have you chosen an appropriate tone:

- Businesslike or bureaucratic?
- Active or passive?
- Jargon or no jargon?

3. Format: Have you used business formats?

See pages 158–165.

Have you used memo, letter, or report formats effectively?

4. Correctness

See pages 167–178.

Have you used correct grammar and punctuation?

CHAPTER V OUTLINE

I. Tell/sell presentations
   1. Preparing what to say
   2. Preparing your notes

II. Questions and answers

III. Consult/join meetings
   1. Preparation before the meeting
   2. Participation during the meeting
   3. Decision making and follow-up

IV. Other speaking situations
   1. Manuscript speaking
   2. Impromptu speaking
   3. Videoconferencing
   4. Dealing with the media
   5. Team presentations

CHAPTER V

Speaking: Verbal Structure

In this chapter, we consider the verbal aspect of speaking—that is, how to structure what you say in various group speaking situations. In Chapters VI and VII, we will look at the two other aspects of presentations: visual aids and nonverbal delivery skills.

Structuring what you say depends on the situation in which you are speaking. The chart that follows illustrates the three kinds of group speaking situations covered in this chapter: (1) tell/sell presentations, (2) questions and answers, and (3) consult/join meetings. This chapter also includes tips for other speaking situations—manuscript speaking, impromptu speaking, videoconferencing, dealing with the media, and team presentations.

SPEAKING: VERBAL STRUCTURE			
Section in this chapter:	**I. Tell/Sell Presentations**	**II. Questions and Answers**	**III. Consult/Join Meetings**
Who speaks most:	You	You to audience	You and audience
Possible purposes:	To inform or to persuade	To answer questions	To discuss or to decide

I. TELL/SELL PRESENTATIONS

SPEAKING: VERBAL STRUCTURE			
Section in this chapter:	**I. Tell/Sell Presentations**	**II. Questions and Answers**	**III. Consult/Join Meetings**
Who speaks most:	You	You to audience	You and audience
Possible purposes:	To inform or to persuade	To answer questions	To discuss or to decide

1. Preparing what to say

If you are speaking to a group of people primarily to inform or persuade them, use these techniques to structure what you say. Presenting information orally differs from presenting it in writing. Therefore, an effective presentation structure includes (1) an opening, (2) a preview of the main points, (3) clearly demarcated main points, and (4) a closing.

Use an effective opening. Openings are important in all forms of communication, as we discussed with the Audience Memory Curve on page 19. When you make an oral presentation, however, your opening is even more crucial than it is when you write. Unlike your readers, who decide when and where to read your document, your listeners have had the time and place imposed on them; they are likely to have other things on their minds. Therefore, always use the first minute or so of your presentation for your opening, what many experts call a "grabber."

To decide what to say during your opening, think about the audience: Are they interested? Do they know how the topic relates to them? Do they know why you're speaking? Do they know you well or not? Given your audience analysis, choose from among the following techniques:

- *Grab their attention.* Why should they listen? Often, your audience will have other things on their minds or will not be especially interested in your topic, so you may need to use what many experts call a "grabber" or a "hook" to arouse their interest. Some common grabbers include a provocative question, a problem definition, a promise of what your presentation will deliver, a personal story that makes a business point, a vivid image, or a striking example or statistic.

- *Show "what's in it for them."* Why should they care? Think about the possible persuasion techniques (from pages 15–17) that might work for this particular audience.
- *Show your main "take-aways."* What will they get out of it? Thinking back to your communication objective (pages 4–5), let them know why you're speaking: (1) what they will learn or your purpose for a tell presentation, or (2) what you hope they will do or your recommendation for a sell presentation. (See pages 19–20 for more on why to use the direct structure.)
- *Build your credibility, if necessary.* Why should they listen to you in particular? Only if your audience doesn't know you, introduce yourself and use any of the techniques discussed on pages 8–9 to enhance your credibility, especially establishing a "common ground."
- *Use humor with caution.* Humor can be an effective grabber; however, use it only if it fits your personality and style, if it is appropriate and inoffensive for every member of the audience, and if it relates to the topic or occasion. Never use humor that might make anyone feel left out, put down, or trivialized.

Next, give a preview. A preview is a table of contents, an agenda, an outline of what you will be covering in your presentation. One of the most common problems in business presentations is the lack of a preview.

Always give an explicit preview before you begin discussing your main points; it will help your audience understand and remember what you say. Think again about the contrast between listeners and readers. Your readers can skim a document, see how long it is, and read your headings and subheadings before they start reading. Your listeners, by contrast, have no idea what you will be covering unless you tell them.

In the most formal situations, a preview might sound like this: "In the next 20 minutes, I will discuss sales in each of three regions: the Southeast, the Far West, and the Midwest." On less formal occasions, your preview might be "I'd like to go over the sales figures in three regions." In any situation, the point of the preview is to give your audience a skeleton view, or general outline, of what you will be discussing.

Typical ways to organize a presentation include a list of: key points (such as reasons, examples, or recommendations), key questions (such as what we are recommending, why we are recommending it, and how we will implement it), or problems and solutions.

State your main points clearly. As noted on pages 38–39, your main points need to be organized and easy to follow. In addition to those general organizational principles, here are three specific techniques to apply to oral presentation structure.

Limit your main points. Be sure to limit the number of main points you make in a presentation, because audiences cannot take in as much through their ears as they can through their eyes. Experiments in cognitive psychology show that people cannot easily comprehend more than five to seven main points. Naturally, this doesn't mean that you say five things and sit down; it means that you should group your complex ideas into five to seven major areas.

Use explicit transitions. When you are speaking, you need longer, more explicit transitions between major sections or subsections than you do when you are writing. Listeners do not stay oriented as easily as readers do; they may not even remember what it is that you are listing unless you use these longer transitions.

Ineffective short transition

Second, . . .

Effective longer transitions

The second recommendation is . . .
Let's move on to the second recommendation.

Use backward look/forward look transitions. In addition to more explicit transitions, you also need to use more repetitive transitions when you're speaking, because listeners may not remember information they hear only once. Inexperienced speakers may feel awkward repeating themselves so much, but remember, it's better for you to feel redundant than for your audience to feel confused. Therefore, between each major section or subsection, use a backward look/forward look transition: the backward look repeats what you've just said; the forward look introduces what you will discuss next.

Effective backward look/forward look

Now that we have looked at the three elements of the marketing plan—modifying the promotion program, increasing direct mail, and eliminating the coupon program **(backward look)**—let's turn to the financial implications of this plan **(forward look)**.

Keep their interest high. In addition to delivering a clear and rational message, remember to keep your audience's attention with an emotionally appealing message. Your audience analysis will drive how much emotion is appropriate, but most business presenters underestimate the importance of emotion. Here are some ways to keep up your audience's interest:

- *Include stories*, case illustrations, analogies, and examples—not just numbers.
- *Incorporate their names* (e.g., "Fatima in accounting and Pat in human resources" instead of "people from different departments").
- *Change your personal energy* (e.g., your tone, pauses, or nonverbal dynamism).
- *Ask rhetorical questions* that relate to audience benefits (e.g., "So what does this mean for your business?").
- *Ask for a show of hands* (e.g., "How many of you think our current policy is effective?).
- *Tell them you'll be asking* for their input after the presentation.

Use an effective closing. Your audience is likely to remember your last words. So don't waste your closing saying something like "Well, that's all I have to say" or "I guess that's about it." Also, don't confuse your audience by introducing a completely new topic.

Instead, use a strong, obvious transitional phrase—such as "to summarize" or "in conclusion"—to introduce your closing remarks. Here are some options for effective closings:

- *Give a summary.* One effective closing is to summarize your main points. You may feel as though you're being repetitive, but this kind of reinforcement is extremely effective when you are explaining or instructing.
- *Arouse their enthusiasm.* Another possibility is to close with a quote, an appeal, or a challenge.
- *Refer to the opening.* A third kind of closing is to refer to the rhetorical question, promise, image, or story you used in your opening.
- *End with the action steps.* You also might choose to end with a call to action based on what you have presented, making the "what next?" step explicit. In addition, you might remind the audience "what's in it for them" if they take these action steps.
- *Concentrate on main ideas.* If you run out of time, do not try to rush through every point. Instead, concentrate on your main points only, especially your summary slide.

2. Preparing your notes

Another aspect of structuring a presentation concerns writing the notes from which you will speak. It's ineffective to turn your back to your audience and read your slides. It's unrealistic to think you can possibly memorize every presentation you make. And you can't interact with your audience if you are reading a word-for-word script.

Therefore, most experts suggest writing your presentation outline on 4- by 6-inch cards. Cards are stiffer and less awkward looking than floppy 8½- by 11-inch pieces of paper and are easier to carry if you want to move. However, use regular-sized paper if that feels more comfortable and looks less awkward for you.

Tips for notecards include:

- *Consider attaching reduced versions of your slides* to your notecards, and then adding in longhand (1) additional notes about what to say, and/or (2) nonverbal reminders (such as "Slow down rate" or "Stand up straight," and/or (3) wording for the backward look/forward look transition between each main section.
- *Use key phrases only:* Do not write out complete sentences; use short headings and phrases only.
- *Make your cards easy to read:* Use big enough lettering so that you can read your notes at arm's length—either handwritten or printed in 14- or 16-point font. Leave lots of white space.
- *Make your main points stand out:* Number and highlight your main points. Use larger letters, bold, or color-coding to differentiate them.
- *Orient the cards "portrait" style:* Most presenters find it easier to keep their place if they are holding a long card rather than a wide one.
- *Don't use too many cards:* Each notecard should contain about five minutes' worth of information.

Now that you have structured your tell/sell presentation, think about the other two components of an effective oral presentation:

- ***Visual aids*** (pages 108–137) and
- ***Nonverbal delivery*** (pages 138–151).

II. QUESTIONS AND ANSWERS

SPEAKING: VERBAL STRUCTURE			
Section in this chapter:	**I. Tell/Sell Presentations**	**II. Questions and Answers**	**III. Consult/Join Meetings**
Who speaks most:	You	You to audience	You and audience
Possible purposes:	To inform or to persuade	To answer questions	To discuss or to decide

Most presentations involve interaction between the speaker and the audience in the form of questions and answers. Dealing effectively with questions and answers involves deciding when to take questions, how to take questions, what to say if you don't know the answer, and how to answer difficult questions.

When to take questions Well before the presentation, think about when you will take questions. Then be sure to inform your audience at the beginning of the presentation. Say, for example, "Please feel free to ask questions as they come up" or "Please hold all your questions until the end of the presentation" or "Feel free to interrupt with questions of understanding or clarification, but since we only have an hour together, please hold questions of debate or discussion until the end."

Usually, audience and cultural expectations are fairly clear: the current trend in most Anglo-American business presentations is to include questions during the presentation; sometimes, however, the norm is for a question-and-answer period at the end of the presentation. If the choice is up to you, think about the following advantages and disadvantages.

Questions after the presentation If you take questions after the presentation, you will maintain control over the schedule and the flow of information. However, you risk (1) losing your audience's attention and perhaps even comprehension if they cannot interrupt with their questions, and (2) placing yourself in an awkward position if important audience members interrupt with questions after you've asked them not to. Because audiences tend to remember more material from the beginning and the end of a presentation, however, having "Q&A" last places undue emphasis on the question period. To alleviate this problem, leave your summary slide displayed during the questions and save time for a two- to three-minute summary after the questions.

Questions during the presentation If you take questions during the presentation, the questions will be more meaningful to the questioner, the feedback will be more immediate, and your audience may listen more actively. However, questions during the presentation can upset your schedule and waste time. To alleviate these problems, (1) allow enough time for questions and (2) control digressions.

How to take questions Once you've established when to take questions, prepare yourself for how you will take them.

Prepare in advance. Prepare yourself by anticipating possible questions. Try to guess what the questions will be. Bring along extra information, perhaps even extra visual aids, to answer such questions if they come up. Another way to anticipate questions is to ask a colleague to play devil's advocate during your rehearsal.

As you prepare, try to control your attitude toward the process. Instead of going in with a defensive attitude, think of it as a compliment if your listeners are interested enough to ask for clarification, amplification, or justification.

Frequently asked questions include those of (1) value ("Are you sure we really need this?" or "What will happen if we don't do this?"), (2) cost ("Can we do it for less?"), (3) action ("How can we do it?" or "Will this action cause new problems?"), and (4) details ("What is your source?" or "Is that number correct?").

Show your understanding. When someone asks a question, listen carefully to be sure you understand it before you answer. Paraphrase or summarize complicated questions to make sure you're on the right track. If the group is large, paraphrase or repeat all questions to be sure everyone in the audience hears them. If someone asks a question you don't understand, say something like "Could you restate that? I'm afraid I don't understand the question," not "Your question isn't clear."

Stick to your objective and your organization. Answer the question, but always keep your communication objective in mind. Even if you have a lot of information for your answer, limit yourself to whatever advances your objective. Don't go off on rambling tangents. If necessary, divert the question back to your main ideas. If someone asks a question you had planned to cover later in your talk, try to answer it in a nutshell and then make it clear that you will cover it in more detail later.

Keep everyone involved. Keep the entire audience involved by calling on people from various locations in the audience and by avoiding a one-to-one conversation with a single member of the audience. When you answer, maintain eye contact with the entire audience, not just with the person who asked the question. Also, avoid ending your answer by looking right at the questioner: he or she may feel invited to ask another question.

What to say if you don't know the answer Sometimes you absolutely don't know the answer; sometimes you don't know the answer without some time to gather your thoughts.

If you don't know If you don't know the answer, say, "I don't know." Even better, suggest where the person might find the answer. Better still, offer to get the answer yourself. For example, "Off the top of my head, I don't know the sales figures for that region, but I'll look them up and have them on your desk by tomorrow morning." Never hazard a guess unless you make it extremely clear that it is only a guess.

If you need some time to think If you are momentarily stymied by a question, here are some techniques to buy you some thinking time: (1) Repeat: "You're wondering how to deal with this situation." (2) Turn the question around: "How would *you* deal with this situation?" (3) Turn the question outward: "How would the rest of you deal with this situation?" (4) Reflect: "Good question. Let's think about that for a moment." (5) Write: If you are using a suitable visual aid, write down the main point of the question as you think.

How to answer difficult questions Some questions are especially challenging because they are confusing, controlling, or hostile.

Confusing questions Confusing questions may be long, rambling, multifaceted, or overly global. In these cases, paraphrase the question before you answer, refocusing to make it appropriate for your communication objective. If the questioner repeats the inappropriately long version of the question, say "I wish we had more time so we could discuss that" or "Let's explore that in more detail after the presentation is over."

Controlling questions Some questions are not really questions; they are statements. In the case of these mini-lectures, do not feel obliged to answer or to ask "So what exactly is your question?" Instead, thank them for their comments, perhaps even paraphrasing their ideas, and then proceed with your presentation.

Other controlling questions are those questions the audience member clearly wants to answer him- or herself or that focus on his or her interests only. In these cases, you need to decide whether you want to (1) regain control yourself by refocusing on your communication objective or (2) change your focus midstream by turning the question back to them ("What do you think we ought to do?"). For example, if you were explaining a new procedure to a large group of employees, you would probably opt to regain control; if you were talking to a small group of important clients, you would probably choose to change focus to meet their needs.

Hostile questions People may be hostile because of lack of information; in these cases, you can influence them through facts and logic. Many times, however, they may be hostile because they feel passionate, threatened, defensive, isolated, or resentful of authority or change. Faced with a hostile question, take a deep breath, identify the hostility ("I understand you feel upset about this"), and answer the question nonemotionally and nonpersonally. Sometimes, you may be able to find a common ground ("We're both trying to do what we feel is in the customer's best interest"). Sometimes, however, you have no choice but to agree to disagree, paraphrasing both points of view clearly.

III. CONSULT/JOIN MEETINGS

SPEAKING: VERBAL STRUCTURE			
Section in this chapter:	**I. Tell/Sell Presentations**	**II. Questions and Answers**	**III. Consult/Join Meetings**
Who speaks most:	You	You to audience	You and audience
Possible purposes:	To inform or to persuade	To answer questions	To discuss or to decide

A third kind of verbal structure is used when you are not presenting information (that is, in tell/sell situations), but rather when you are eliciting information from others (that is, in consult/join situations). In reality, we all know that some meetings include presentations and reports and that some presentations turn into free-for-all discussions. However, for the purposes of explaining interactive versus presentational skills, let's assume that in a meeting you are trying to elicit group feedback rather than to present your own ideas.

Many businesspeople erroneously assume that running a meeting is easy, simple, and straightforward. Actually, meetings involve a complex and difficult set of tasks. According to negotiation expert Lindsay Rahmun, meetings are difficult because of a set of inherent contradictions she dubs "the participant's dilemma": we expect people to be thoughtful and innovative, yet simultaneously fast and efficient; we are annoyed when people don't participate, yet annoyed when they talk too much; we expect people to offer their best ideas, yet not get defensive when those ideas are modified or rejected; we want to hold high standards of quality and resist "groupthink," yet at the same time we call people stubborn and inflexible if they don't move with the group; we want to work with a small group for efficiency, yet with a large group for inclusiveness.

Following are some guidelines for dealing with three complex sets of issues: (1) preparation before the meeting, (2) participation during the meeting, and (3) decision making and follow-up after the meeting. For more techniques for meeting management, see the book, *Guide to Meetings*, listed on page 182 of the bibliography.

1. Preparation before the meeting

Before the meeting, think carefully about the meeting objective, agenda, and roles.

Set the objective. Perhaps the single most prevalent complaint about meetings is that they are called unnecessarily. Meetings should be reserved for situations in which you need group discussion, not for routine announcements or for presenting your own finalized ideas.

Set the agenda. Because the whole purpose of a meeting is to elicit information from other people, prepare your agenda carefully and in advance, so that participants can think of ideas ahead of time.

- *Think about meeting length.* Remember that productivity tends to drop after about two hours or if you have too many topics to cover.
- *State the purpose* clearly on the agenda, and again at the beginning of the meeting.
- *State the purpose for each agenda item.* Then, for each item on the agenda, answer the following questions for the participants: (1) What is the purpose of each agenda item? Clearly differentiate items that are "for your information," "for discussion," or "for a decision." (2) What is your tentative timing for each topic? (3) How should they prepare? Include any background information with the agenda.
- *Clarify participant preparation.* Let participants know how they should prepare and how they will be expected to contribute—for example, "Think about the pros and cons of this proposal" or "List five ideas before the meeting."

Delegate roles. Decide what role(s) you are going to perform yourself—and which you will delegate to someone else.

- *Facilitator:* If you have strong feelings about the subject at hand or want to participate actively, you should consider asking someone else to facilitate the discussion.
- *Timer:* You may wish to appoint someone else to serve as timekeeper, because it's hard to concentrate on the discussion and keep your mind on the time all at once.

- *Minutes writer:* You may also want to appoint someone else to write up minutes after the meeting, to check the minutes before they are distributed, and to decide who will receive a copy of the minutes.
- *Scribe:* Finally, instead of choosing to record participant comments during the meeting yourself, consider asking someone else to serve as scribe.

  This increasingly popular technique (1) *makes you more effective* because you can face and maintain connection with the audience instead of trying to write and talk at the same time; (2) *improves legibility* and possibly accuracy because the scribe has more time to write carefully; and (3) *increases meeting energy* while saving meeting time because you can go on to discuss the next point while the scribe is still recording the previous point.

2. Participation during the meeting

Here are some techniques to increase participation.

Opening the meeting At the beginning of the meeting, plan to:

- *Set the tone.* Start on time. Get people interested, involved, and enthusiastic by giving a short introduction and then involving them early.
- *Explain the agenda.* Make sure everyone understands and agrees on the meeting's purpose, impetus, agenda, and decision-making technique.
- *Get people to agree on ground rules.* Meetings will run much more effectively if everyone agrees explicitly on the ground rules at the outset. If you wait until someone has erred before you clarify the rules, the person will feel humiliated. If, however, you have the rules clear from the start, a brief reminder will usually work.

  Examples of ground rules include the following: We will start and stop on time. We will not interrupt. We will stick to the agenda. We will treat all information as confidential.
- *Involve people early.* The earlier you can get participants involved in some way, the more likely they are to participate. If you are dealing with a passive or quiet group, you might think of some activity or icebreaker that involves them early in the session.

During the meeting Throughout the meeting, use the listening skills explained on pages 152–155 to encourage everybody's participation.

- *Ask open-ended questions.* Ask questions that cannot be answered "yes" or "no," such as "What are your reactions to this proposal?" or "How should we attack this problem?"
- *Paraphrase their responses.* Restate their ideas accurately and concisely, to let them know they've been heard, such as "So what you're suggesting is . . ."
- *Record their responses.* Either you or your scribe should record participants' ideas on a board or chart in full public view (1) *accurately,* paraphrasing essential phrases only, (2) *inclusively,* including everybody's input, and (3) *readably,* using large, dark, neat lettering.
- *Use "minimal encouragers."* Use minimal encouragers—such as "I see," "OK," or "uh huh"—to keep the discussion going.
- *Handle disagreement carefully.* Do not show your disagreement too soon (e.g., "That won't work because" or "I disagree because"). State disagreements carefully: disagree with ideas, not with people personally.
- *Avoid dominance by any one person or subgroup.* Draw in all people; use a firm but tactful reminder of the ground rules; or talk to disruptive, very verbal, or high-status people privately before or after the meeting to avoid a direct confrontation in front of the group.
- *Don't talk too much.* It is hard to avoid dominating a meeting you are running. You have decided to call a meeting; therefore, don't deliver a lecture or presentation.

3. Decision making and follow-up

Don't waste the valuable ideas you gained from the meeting participants; use the following techniques to make a decision and to follow up.

Decision making For those items on your agenda that require a decision, make it clear to the participants in advance which decision-making method you plan to use.

- *By one person or majority vote:* These two methods are quite fast and are effective when the decision is not particularly important or when you face severe time constraints. Their disadvantage, however, is that some people may feel left out, ignored, or defeated—and these people may later sabotage the implementation.
- *By consensus:* Consensus means reaching a compromise that may not be everybody's first choice but that each person is willing to agree on and implement. Consensus involves hearing all points of view and incorporating these viewpoints into the solution, so it is time consuming and requires group commitment to the process. Unlike majority rule, consensus is reached by discussion, not by a vote. For example, the facilitator might ask "Do you all feel comfortable with this solution?" or "Seems to me we've reached consensus around this idea. Am I right?" Consensus does not mean unanimity; no participant has veto power.

Follow-up How you end the meeting can be the most crucial key to success: all the time and effort spent on the meeting itself will be wasted if no one acts on the ideas. At the close of the meeting, take the time to figure out how you are going to follow up with a permanent record and an action plan.

- *Permanent record:* Most meetings should be documented with a permanent record of some kind, usually called the "minutes," to record what occurred and to communicate those results. Effective minutes include the issues discussed, the alternatives considered, the decisions reached, and the action plan. Eventually, participants should receive hard or electronic copy of the minutes and the action plan.
- *Action plan:* The group should agree to an action plan, to include (1) what actions are to be taken, (2) who is responsible for each action, (3) the time frame for each action, and (4) how the action will be reported back to the group. A good way to start your next meeting might be to present an update on the previous meeting's action plan.

IV. OTHER SPEAKING SITUATIONS

In addition to the three standard speaking situations already covered in this chapter, you may find yourself in other kinds of situations. This section offers some additional techniques for dealing with (1) manuscript speaking, (2) impromptu speaking, (3) videoconferencing, (4) dealing with the media, and (5) team presentations.

1. Manuscript speaking The tell/sell presentations discussed in the first section of this chapter use notes, but are not read word for word. You may find, however, that you are occasionally called upon to speak word for word from a manuscript.

Use "spoken style." The main problem people have in writing manuscript speeches is that they use "written style" instead of "spoken style." A speech in written style may look fine on paper, but when delivered, it sounds stilted, formal, and pompous. When you write a manuscript speech, then, keep in mind four aspects of spoken style: (1) *Avoid phrases no one would actually say,* phrases that sound stilted or are hard to pronounce. For example, you might write, "If you were asked to do so," but you would say, "If someone asked you to do that." (2) *Avoid phrases separating the subject from the verb.* Your reader can easily follow this sentence: "Maria Martinez, who is currently the president of ABC Company, will be the first speaker on the panel." You make it much easier for the listener, however, if you do not separate the subject from the verb: "President Maria Martinez will be the first speaker on the panel." (3) *Use shorter sentences.* Speech writing generally uses shorter sentences and sometimes even sentence fragments. (4) *Remember that rhythm is much more important* in spoken style than in written style. Consider, for example, the rhythmic impact of Patrick Henry's famous quotation "Give me liberty or give me death." Similarly, John Kennedy's rhythmic "Ask not what your country can do for you; ask what you can do for your country" is more effective than the unrhythmic "Don't ask what your country can do for you, but what you can do for it."

Write and edit. Keeping the preceding four considerations in mind, write the first draft of your speech, or write notes and then record yourself speaking from those notes. The transcript of what you just recorded becomes the draft of the speech. Once you have a draft, edit it and then read it aloud (or have the person for whom you're writing the speech read it aloud). After making any necessary changes, you are ready to type the manuscript in its final form.

Prepare the manuscript. A speech manuscript looks different from a regular page of writing. For one thing, it should be typed in a large font. The margins also look strange: leave about one third of the right side of the page blank for notes; leave about one third at the bottom of the page blank so that your head will not drop too low as you read. Because it is awkward to read a sentence that starts on one page and finishes on the next, never break a sentence between two pages. In fact, many speech experts suggest never breaking even a paragraph between two pages. Never staple the pages of a speech; the speaker should be able to slide the page to one side. Finally, many speakers underline key words for vocal emphasis.

2. Impromptu speaking Impromptu speaking means talking on the spur of the moment, without advance preparation. For example, your boss may suddenly ask you to "bring us up to date on a certain service." Usually, of course, you will not be asked to make impromptu remarks unless you have some knowledge in the area.

Here are some suggestions to help you in impromptu speaking situations: (1) *Anticipate*. Try to avoid truly impromptu situations. Guess at the probability of your being called on during discussions, meetings, or interviews. Guess at the topics you might be asked to discuss. (2) *Relate to experience*. You will speak more easily and confidently if you try to relate the topic to your specific experiences and to the topics you know best. (3) *Keep your remarks short*. Say what you have to say and then stop. Do not ramble on, feeling that you must deliver a lengthy lecture. (4) *Organize as well as you can*. If you have a few seconds, jot down your main points (e.g., past/present/future, advantages/disadvantages, or reasons for/reasons against). Then, stick to these main points, avoiding tangents. (5) *End strongly*. At the end, summarize your main takeaways.

3. Videoconferencing Videoconferencing can be used in situations ranging from collaborative meetings to corporate town meetings to distance learning. The venue can also range from large rooms, board rooms, or small rooms to individual desktop monitors.

Videoconferencing has many advantages: reaching a geographically dispersed audience in multiple locations simultaneously; saving on travel time and money; allowing you to see people and gauge their responses; allowing for collaboration by using document sharing; and reaching extremely large audiences, far more people than can fit into any one room.

You can gain many of the same advantages, however, by using audioconferencing (typically called "conference calls"). So, choose conference calls unless you really need to see the audience. Conference calls will save money, add scheduling flexibility, and decrease your chances for technical glitches.

When using videoconferencing, keep in mind the following guidelines.

Plan the conference.

- Set the objective and agenda; select and invite participants; distribute materials in advance; prepare graphics and visual aids. (See pages 97–101 for meeting details.)
- Assign a leader for each site. Get a phone number to call if the conference suddenly disconnects.
- Work around multiple time zones and arrange for translators or a taped archival copy, if appropriate.
- Rehearse in advance; practice with keypad or other equipment if necessary; critique yourself on tape.
- Send your slides or documents electronically to other sites ahead of time.

Plan with the technician.

- Before the day of the conference, have your technician do a "tech check," connecting to the other site(s) to make sure everything connects and is compatible. As part of that tech check, (1) think about how both the speaker(s) and the slides will be shown, (2) discuss camera angles (try to arrange for close-ups of the person talking instead of a long shot of everyone in the room), and (3) check the sound for volume and lack of echoes.

- Make sure you know how to deal with the slide projector or document camera, mute the sound, and change camera angles during the conference.
- Arrange to have a technician (1) come in right before the conference to recheck the equipment and (2) be on call during the conference—either in the room or nearby—to deal with technical glitches. Make sure you have the telephone numbers of the technicians at the other sites as well.

Work effectively with people and slides.

- Ask people to introduce themselves (e.g., "This is Laurie MacGregor in Oregon").
- Make sure someone in each location knows how to display the slides so you are all looking at the same visual at the same time.
- "Introduce" each slide, as explained on page 133.

Enhance your body language.

- Be yourself; look confident; don't be afraid to smile; talk to participants as if they were sitting across from you.
- Maintain eye contact by looking straight into the camera.
- Avoid any quick movements; use slow, restrained hand gestures; avoid any quirky mannerisms, such as fiddling with your glasses or tapping your pen.
- Assume you're always "on stage": avoid side conversations; sit naturally, neither stone-still nor squirming.
- Tend to your appearance, as described on the next page.

Enhance your voice.

- Speak naturally and conversationally, with pauses and inflection. However, speak a bit more slowly, more deliberately, and more loudly than usual, without shouting.
- Avoid unwanted sounds: coughing into microphone, tapping your fingers or pencil near microphone, breathing heavily, rattling papers, or jingling coins.
- Remember to pause so that others may speak.

For more on how to dress, see the following page. For more on running meetings, see pages 97–101.

4. Dealing with the media Here are some techniques to use for media interviews.

Preparing in advance

- *Cultivate and maintain media relationships.* (1) Get to know the reporters who cover your industry and company. (2) Find out about the reporters who are interviewing you. Look at their previous stories or watch previous shows—watching for their biases; favorite themes; interview formats; and use of charts, graphs, or bullet points. Prepare information the way they prefer to receive it.
- *Analyze two audiences.* Analyze both the reporter and the end users (that is, the readers or viewers).
- *Think of questions in advance.* If possible, find out in advance from the reporters what topics or questions they intend to ask. In addition, brainstorm possible questions: If you were the reporter, what would you ask? What would the audience be interested in? Ask colleagues and potential audience members to brainstorm questions.
- *Plan your responses in advance.* Think about what you want to communicate, what main messages you want to get across. Structure these messages into short, crisp statements.

Responding during the interview

- *Listen carefully.* Think before responding. Answer only the question you were asked.
- *Use "bridging"* to move from the reporters' questions to your main messages.
- *Bring your points to life* by using short anecdotes, analogies, and simple statistics.

Being on camera

- *Prepare for mechanical distractions.* Rehearse on set to learn cues and see the equipment.
- *Decide where to focus.* If you are recording by yourself, you will probably look directly at the camera; if you are appearing on a talk show, you will probably look at the host.
- *Dress appropriately.* (1) Wear light-colored clothing (not white) and solid colors, such as blue, gray, teal, or pastels. (2) Avoid plaids, patterns, prints, black, red, and the color of the backdrop. (3) Keep jewelry subtle and simple.

For more information on dealing with the media, see the *Guide to Media Relations*, cited in the bibliography, page 182.

5. Team presentations Make sure your team presentations are organized, unified, and coherent—not simply an unrelated series of individual presentations.

Organize as a whole. The major problem with team presentations occurs when each presenter prepares a separate part, and the parts never coalesce into a coherent whole. To avoid this problem, compose the agenda before you even think about who will say what. In other words, structure the agenda by the appropriate number of content areas, not by the number of members you happen to have in your team. After the agenda is completed, then decide the speaking order, remembering that one speaker may cover two content sections, or one content section may be covered by multiple speakers.

Provide content transitions between speakers. To begin, one team member should provide the opening and preview for the presentation as a whole, introducing the team members and the topics they will cover. Then, after each speaker finishes, he or she should provide a backward look/forward look transition (as explained on page 90), such as "Now that I have explained our proposal (**backward look**), Tyrone will explain the financial implications of that proposal (**forward look**)."

Use visual aids consistently. Your visuals should look team designed, not individually designed. (1) Use the same template or overall design throughout (e.g., the same colors, fonts, and sizes, as covered on pages 110–117). (2) Interact with your visuals consistently (e.g., how you use the remote or animation, as explained on pages 132–137.)

Rehearse and deliver as a group. In your first run-through—or what speaking expert Antony Jay calls the "stagger-through"—practice what you will say, the exact wording of your transitions, and rough drafts of your visuals. In a second run-through, work to perfect your delivery and flow.

Choreograph your logistics. Remember that you are all "on stage" from the moment you walk in the room. Therefore (1) *Plan exactly* how you will start, seat the nonspeakers, "hand off" to one another, finish, and take questions (Who will moderate and direct questions? How will you sit?). (2) *Maintain professional nonverbal behavior* while others speak: look attentive and avoid side conversations.

CHAPTER VI OUTLINE

I. Designing the presentation as a whole
   1. Translate your structure into draft slides.
   2. Connect the agenda and the backup slides.
   3. Choose colors for your Slide Master.
   4. Choose typography for your Slide Master.
   5. Use animation to "build" your ideas.

II. Designing each individual slide
   1. Using message titles
   2. Designing graphs to show "how much"
   3. Designing concept diagrams to show "how"
   4. Designing word charts to show "why" or "how"
   5. Editing each slide

III. Choosing visual aid equipment

IV. Practicing with visual aids
   1. General preparation techniques
   2. Techniques for specific equipment

CHAPTER VI

Speaking: Visual Aids

No matter how well you have prepared what you are going to say (Chapter V) or how skilled you may be in your nonverbal speaking delivery (Chapter VII), your audience still has the capacity to daydream: they can think faster than you can speak. To keep them concentrating on your ideas, provide visual aids that back up what you're saying. Visual aids . . .

- *Add* interest, variety, and impact.
- *Increase audience comprehension* and retention.
- *Remain in the memory* longer than just words.
- *Reach 40% of your audience* who are likely to be visual, rather than auditory, learners.

Here are some techniques to use for (1) designing the visual presentation as a whole, (2) designing each individual slide, (3) choosing the equipment, and (4) using visuals effectively.

VISUAL AIDS			
I. Designing the presentation as a whole	II. Designing each individual slide	III. Choosing visual aid equipment	IV. Practicing with visual aids

I. DESIGNING THE PRESENTATION AS A WHOLE

VISUAL AIDS			
I. Designing the presentation as a whole	II. Designing each individual slide	III. Choosing visual aid equipment	IV. Practicing with visual aids

This section describes a five-step process for designing your visuals for the entire presentation. Think through these macro issues first, before you start composing individual slides, as described in Part II, the second main section of this chapter.

1. Translate your structure into draft slides.

The first step is to translate your presentation structure (as discussed on pages 88–91) into draft slides.

Opening → slide optional When you are grabbing your audience's interest (pages 88–89), you can display a (1) *blank screen* to keep the spotlight on you and your words, rather than on a competing visual; (2) *title slide*, visually reinforcing the subject of the presentation; or (3) *opening slide(s)*—such as a striking photograph, quotation, or statistic—to help arouse your audience's interest.

Preview → agenda slide Your preview should definitely be displayed on an agenda slide. This agenda slide is perhaps the most important slide in your presentation. It serves as your presentation's "table of contents"; the rest of the slides in the presentation are like the chapters amplifying each idea in this table of contents. Therefore, make sure your agenda slide (1) *makes stand-alone sense* of the key takeaways, as explained on page 52 and as shown on the facing page; (2) *repeats the presentation title in its title*, also shown in the example at right; (3) *ties to the backup slides* by using the same or very similar wording for your backup slides' titles as you did for your agenda slide's main points; (4) *ties to the summary slide* by making them clearly parallel, or even identical, to one another. In fact, consider composing your summary slide first, then your agenda slide—or at least revising your agenda slide once you have composed your summary slide—so you are sure they tie together and are both organized around key takeaways.

Ineffective agenda slide

Agenda
• Overview
• Product
• Market Analysis
• Competition
• Operations
• Summary

Title lacks "stand-alone sense"
Unnecessary on agenda slide
Not conceptually parallel
Bullets lack "stand-alone sense"

Effective agenda slide

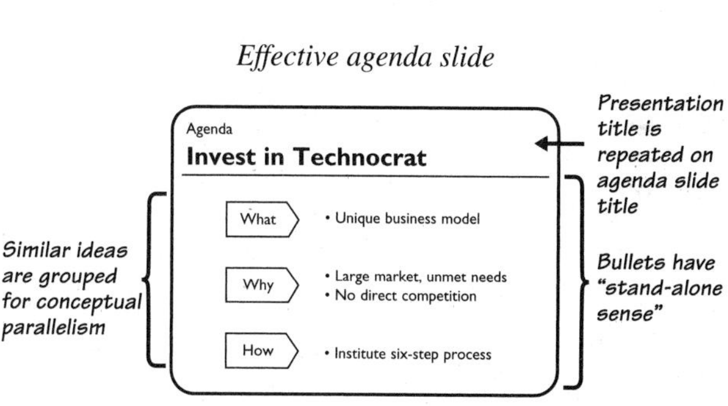

Main points → backup slides Backup slides explain, or "back up," each point on the agenda. Therefore, (1) prepare one or more backup slides to explain each agenda item, and (2) make sure all of your backup slides follow from, and relate back to, the agenda—as explained on pages 112–113.

Closing → summary slide Along with the agenda slide, your summary slide is the most important slide in your presentation. Therefore, ensure that your summary slide (1) includes the main takeaways, (2) is similar—or identical—to your agenda slide, and (3) remains visible during your question and answer session.

2. Connect the agenda and the backup slides.

Throughout the presentation, you need to keep your audience reminded of where you are on your agenda, so they can keep anchored to the main points at all times. Here are three options for doing so.

Consistency One easy but powerful technique for connection is to use scrupulous consistency.

- *Same wording:* Make sure that the slide heading in each backup slide uses exactly the same wording you used in the agenda. For example, if your agenda says "Increase product innovation," your backup slide should use exactly that wording—not similar wording like "Innovate for new products."
- *Same numbering system:* If the points are numbered in the agenda, use the same numbering system in your backup slides.

Repeated agenda Another effective technique is to display your agenda slide repeatedly throughout the presentation, each time you switch to the next main section in your agenda. When you repeat your agenda, use some method to emphasize the upcoming section, such as . . .

- *Highlight the text* of the upcoming section in a different color.
- *Put a box* around the text of the upcoming section.
- *Insert an arrow* pointing to the upcoming section.

Examples of repeated agendas

Improve Growth and Efficiency for Bard Company

1. Target specific customer segments.
2. **Consolidate operations.**
3. Change product mix.

Improve Growth and Efficiency for Bard Company

1. Target specific customer segments.
2. Consolidate operations. (boxed)
3. Change product mix.

Trackers If your presentation is especially long or complex, consider using "trackers" on each backup slide. Trackers serve the same purpose as the "running header" at the top of the pages of this and other books—that is, reminding the audience what section you are currently discussing.

- *What they are:* Trackers are a shortened version of each main point on the agenda, with each point reduced to one or two words.
- *Where they appear:* As shown in the following examples, trackers usually appear in the upper left corner; the lower right corner; or across the bottom of the slide—where they are visible, but not emphatic (e.g., in a smaller font and muted color). Do not use a tracker on the title, agenda, or summary slides.

Tracker
Heading heading heading
• Bullet text bullet text
• Bullet text bullet text
• Bullet text bullet text

Heading heading heading
• Bullet text bullet text
• Bullet text bullet text
• Bullet text bullet text
Tracker

Heading heading heading
• Bullet text bullet text
• Bullet text bullet text
• Bullet text bullet text
Tracker 1 • Tracker 2 • Tracker 3

- *What they look like:* If you used a diagram as an agenda, you might use a miniversion of it as a tracker; however, do not introduce such a diagram if you didn't introduce it in your agenda.
- *What they include:* The tracker can include either (1) the point you're currently discussing only (as shown in the first two examples above), or (2) all of your main points, with the current point highlighted in a different color (as shown in the third example above).

3. Choose colors for your Slide Master.

Once you have a draft (or "storyboard") of your slides, it's time to translate your draft slides into a computer slideware program such as PowerPoint. The trick is to take charge of and maintain control of PowerPoint—instead of (1) boring your audience by scanning in a word document and reading it aloud, or (2) distracting them by using every special effect and clicking every button you can find.

First of all, unless your company prescribes one, take charge of your template (or Slide Master). Alas, virtually all PowerPoint templates are inappropriate for business presentations because they have intrusive backgrounds (with shading, shimmering, 3D effects, etc.), are full of unnecessary decorative items, and draw too much attention to themselves. Or, in the words of PowerPoint critic Edward Tufte, "No matter how beautiful your PP readymade template is, it would be better if there were less of it."

Instead, design your template and then stick with that design (not just in terms of color, but also in terms of size, font, titles, text, trackers, etc.) throughout the entire presentation.

Choose a solid background. Use a solid color without patterns, shimmers, textures, or fades that may make your text unreadable.

- *For a computer projector* in a darkened room: Pick a cool color—like bright blue, green, or maroon—for the background because cool colors appear to recede on screen. Most viewers find the glare of a plain white background in a darkened room distracting.
- *For an overhead projector* in a well-lit room: Choose a light background color—such as a pale blue or clear.

Choose a sharply contrasting foreground color. Your foreground color—the color used for titles and text—should contrast sharply with your background color. The key is to test the colors to make sure that they contrast sharply when projected on the large screen, not just as they appear on your computer monitor.

- *For a computer projector,* generally pick a warm color for the foreground color, because warm colors appear to "pop out" from a dark background. Good choices would include a bright yellow foreground color against a bright blue or green background, or a black foreground against a light green or blue background. Avoid red, green, or light yellow against a dark background.

- *For an overhead projector,* good choices would include a black or dark blue foreground color on clear or white backgrounds. Avoid yellow or orange on overheads.
- *For slide titles versus text:* You also may want to choose different colors to differentiate the slide titles from the slide text. Similarly, you might choose a different background color for the slide title area or a line separating the title from the text.

Choose an accent color. In addition to your basic color template, choose a bright, contrasting color for your accent color (sometimes known as "spot color")—that is, color used occasionally to lead your viewers' eyes to a particular place for emphasis.

- *Use for special emphasis* on some slides—such as an emphatic arrow or highlighted section.
- *Do not use accent color for unemphatic elements:* Your viewers' eyes will be drawn first to anything shown in your accent color, so don't use accent color for unimportant items, such as the line separating the title from the text or the actual bullet points themselves.
- *Avoid the "fruit salad effect."* Effective use of accent color is the opposite of what design expert Jan White has dubbed the "fruit salad effect"—such as a pie chart with every piece of the pie a different color or a column chart with every column a different color. White points out that "the more colors there are, the more difficult it is to remember the meaning each carries. Keep the code simple." He sees four distinct colors as the maximum. For much more information on use of color, see his book, *Color for Impact*, listed on page 182.
- *Keep in mind cultural and physical issues.* Remember that emotional overtones of color vary by culture—for example, the color associated with death, with the country's flag, or with an organization's corporate identity will have special meaning for that organization. Also remember that 8% of men and 1% of women are color-blind, so avoid using green and red as contrasting colors. Blue is a universally recognized color.
- *Tie to your message titles:* Finally, use your accent color to emphasize the data that reinforces your message title, as illustrated on page 120.

4. Choose typography for your Slide Master.

In addition to your template colors, think about your template typography, which includes font size and type, case, and emphatic typography.

Large enough letters For a large-screen presentation, use about 28–32 point for titles, 18–24 point for text, and 14 point for labels. Once you have chosen your font size, use that size consistently (e.g., do not downsize the font on one of titles so you can fit more words into the space).

Unserifed font For large-screen presentations, use an unserifed (or "sans serif") font—that is, a font without extenders (or "feet") on the ends of each letter stroke. Reserve serif fonts—which have these extenders, like the one you are reading right now—for hard copy, with its higher resolution. Unserifed fonts, on the other had, are generally more readable in electric form because of the lower resolution on screen. Some studies show that Verdana is the most readable font on screen; Arial is another good choice for an unserifed font.

Readable case Choose from three kinds of "case": sentence, title, or all capitals.

- *Use sentence case for all text.* In sentence case, only the first letter of the phrase or sentence is capitalized, as in a normal sentence.

  This is sentence case. Use it for your text in each slide.

- *Use title case for titles only.* In title case, the first letter of every word is capitalized. Use title case for your presentation title. For your headings on each individual slide, choose sentence case flush to the left margin (more contemporary and prevalently used) or title case centered (more traditional).

  This Is Title Case. Avoid Using Title Case For Text Because Title Case Causes Pointless Bumps Which Slow Down Your Reader.

- *Avoid all capitals:* Avoid using all capital letters, because they are harder to read, as shown here.

  AVOID ALL CAPITALS, ESPECIALLY WITH UNSERIFED FONT LIKE THIS ONE. THE LACK OF SIZE VARIATION WITH ALL CAPS AND NO EXTENDERS ON THE LETTERS MAKES THIS COMBINATION THE HARDEST TO READ.

Emphatic typography Think about how you will use typography for emphasis (such as boldface and italics).

Good examples of typography

You might choose bold for titles

You might choose italics for subtitles

Bad examples of typography

DO NOT OVERUSE TYPOGRAPHY (bold + all caps + underlining)

Do not use hard-to-read typography (shadow style)

Do not USE *jarring* font *variations* (usually, use one font only)

5. Use animation to "build" your ideas.

Custom animation is one of the key advantages PowerPoint offers. This tool allows you to "build"—that is, systematically disclose—one idea at a time so you can keep the audience focused on the point you are currently making. If you don't use animation, and simply display the entire slide at once, the audience may read ahead, or become confused or distracted figuring out which point you are discussing.

Therefore, think about the best ways to use this function.

Build important bullet text. Your listeners will always read ahead of what you are discussing. Therefore, use build on any slide you need to go through slowly, such as your agenda slide, and any slide on which you will be talking for a fair amount of time on each point.

Build complex graphs. If you display a complex graph all at once, your listeners will be trying to figure out how your graph works instead of listening to you. Therefore, build the slide gradually, explaining each new element as you add it.

Avoid animation "effects." PowerPoint offers a variety of animation effects and sounds—such as flying, dissolving, dropping down, swiveling, wiping, and even checkerboarding. Such excessive animation, with text or graphics flying in from every side and spinning around, distracts your audience. Therefore, choose the "Appear" effect, in which your next point simply appears all at once.

For much more information about PowerPoint, see *Guide to PowerPoint*, cited on page 182.

II. DESIGNING EACH INDIVIDUAL SLIDE

VISUAL AIDS			
I. Designing the presentation as a whole	II. Designing each individual slide	III. Choosing visual aid equipment	IV. Practicing with visual aids

Once you have planned your presentation as a whole, described in the previous section, then design each individual chart. This section covers design techniques to do so: (1) using message titles, (2) designing graphs, (3) designing concept diagrams, (4) designing word charts, and (5) editing each slide.

1. Using message titles

The first thing that each individual slide should have is a "message title"—that is, a main heading or "headline" that summarizes the key takeaway of that particular slide. The message title should make sense to someone reading it for the first time; put yourself in the shoes of someone who arrived at your presentation late or someone who missed the presentation and is reading copies of your slides. Let's take a look at an ineffective title, then some more effective examples.

Avoid topic titles. Ineffective presenters use topic titles—that is, titles that simply state the subject of the slide, but don't tell the viewer what message to take away. For example, as visuals guru Gene Zelazny points out in *Say It with Charts*, given the following slide with a topic title only, your audience might perceive any one of the following messages: (1) the number of contracts has increased, (2) the number of contracts is fluctuating, (3) the number of contracts peaked in August, or (4) the number of contracts declined in two of the last eight months.

Example: ineffective topic title

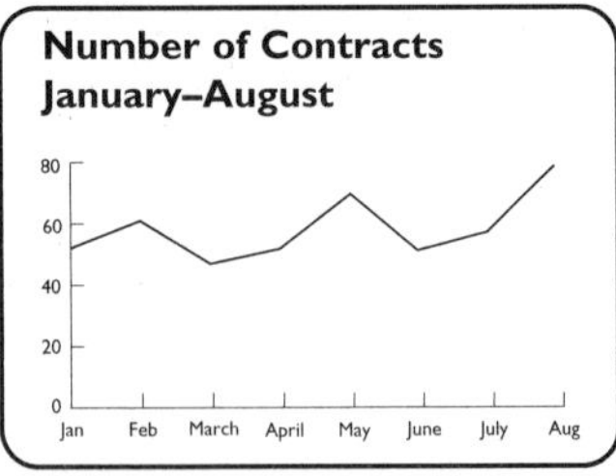

Generally, use a topic title only when you have no message. For example, you may ask your audience to discuss what they observe in the data presented in the slide.

Use message titles. Usually, however, in business presentations, you have a message your want to get across. So make that message clear to your audience by using a message title—that is, a short phrase or sentence with a point to it. Here are some more examples; they are shown as slides on the following page.

Ineffective topics titles:	*Effective message titles:*
Company rankings	Company B ranks second.
Use of materials	Product C uses less graphite.
Sales over time	Sales declined in March.
Share of profits	East generates the smallest share of profits.

Consider the benefits of message titles. Message titles offer many important benefits, to both you and your audience.

- *Improve audience comprehension.* The audience will understand your visuals better because they see the main point easily.
- *Save processing time.* The audience can also process your visuals more quickly, thus speeding up the information–sharing process.
- *Help you with transitions.* Message titles also can make transitions easier for you, especially if they provide a link from one visual to the next. (See page 90 for more on the oral wording of transitions.)
- *Improve decks or handouts.* Message titles are especially helpful to make sure your audience grasps your main points if they are reading them—after the presentation or for the first time—in written form.

Use one title only. Each slide should make one main point, and that main point should be stated in larger typeface at the top of your slide. Therefore, (1) avoid placing your main message as a key takeaway at the bottom of the slide, for all the reasons discussed under the direct approach (pages 19–20); and (2) avoid having one title on the top of the slide and a second title on the top of an imported graph. (In other words, do not enter a graph title into a graph you're going to import.)

Use a message title in your agenda and summary slides. As we discussed on pages 110–111, avoid titles such as "Agenda" or "Summary." Instead, repeat your presentation title on both of those slides, along with the words "agenda" or "summary."

MESSAGE TITLES AND ACCENT COLOR

1. Accent color alone

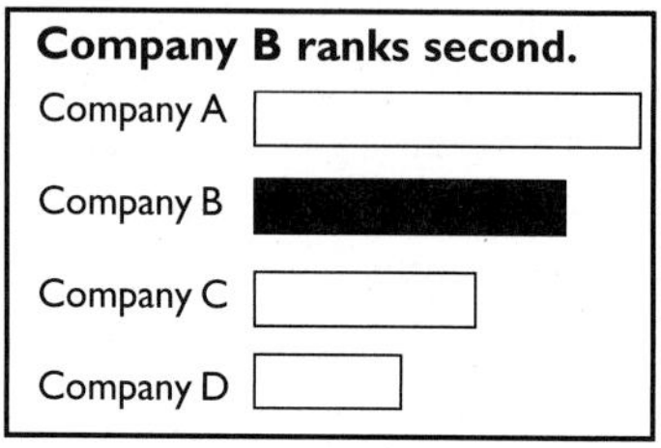

2. With lines

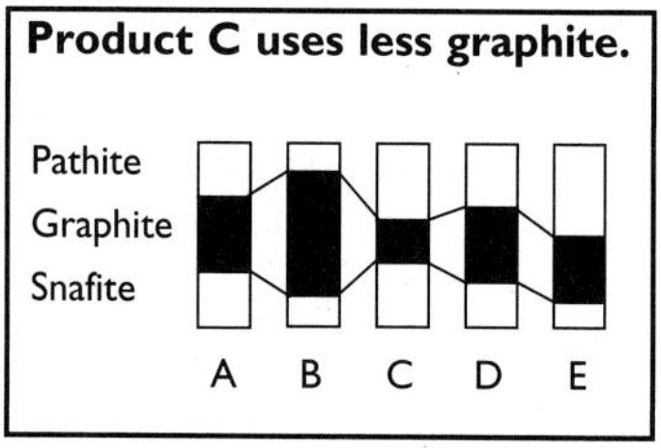

3. With arrows

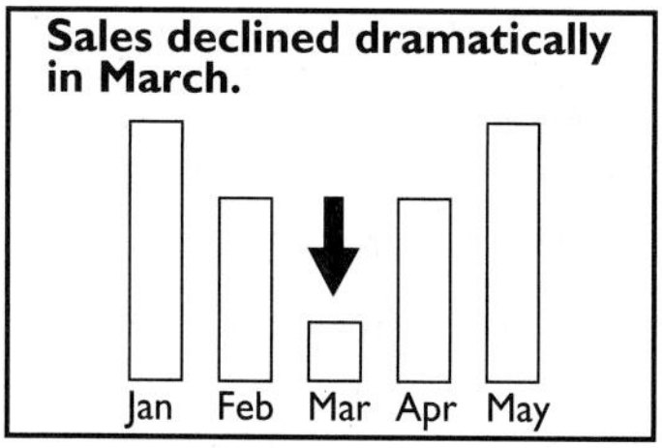

4. With "exploded" off section

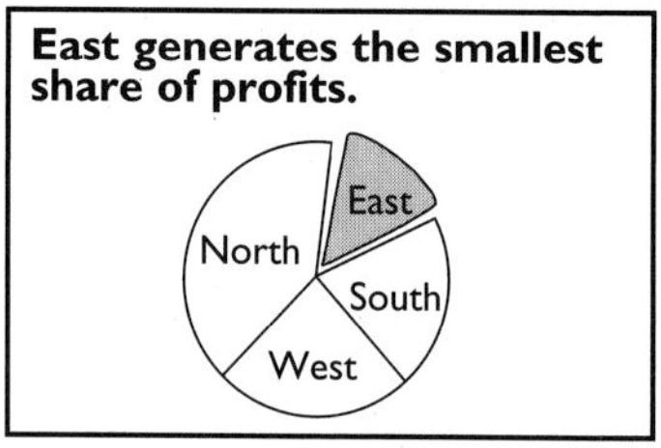

2. Designing graphs to show "how much"

Business presentations often include quantitative data, such as financial information, marketing projections, or operations analyses. In many cases, this kind of data will be easier to comprehend and retain if you show it on graphs (such as line charts or bar charts) rather than just in words and figures (such as lists, tabular charts, spreadsheets, or financial statements).

Examples: table doesn't show trend; graph does

2005		2006	
January	12,543	January	16,985
February	14,371	February	16,106
March	15,998	March	15,422
April	15,004	April	15,010
May	15,281	May	14,564
June	15,742	June	13,820
July	16,101	July	12,489
August	16,254	August	11,376
September	16,378	September	10,897
October	16,495	October	10,178
November	16,397	November	9,657
December	16,463	December	9,281

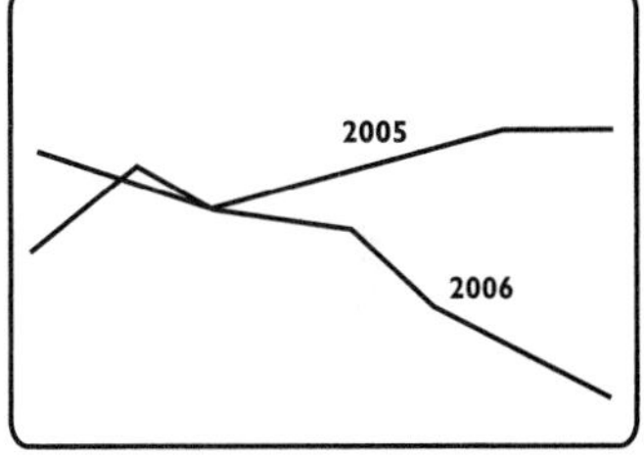

Choosing a graph To show quantitative data graphically, choose from among the most prevalent graph types, shown on the following page. In addition to those shown, other graph types include grouped line graphs (with more than one line), grouped bar graphs (with more than one bar for each item), sliding bar graphs (with a line down the middle of the page and bars on the positive and negative sides), and various other combinations.

Choosing among graph options Keep the following tips in mind if you have the choice between two graphs, as shown on the following page.

- *Line versus column to show time:* Choose a line graph to show trends or an extensive number of time periods; choose a column to emphasize one particular column or show extreme variability.
- *Bar versus column to compare items:* Prefer bar graphs in general, because they are horizontal and therefore labels fit more easily, and because columns may imply a time sequence.
- *Ordering items:* Think about the ordering of the individual items (bars, columns, lines, etc.). Put them in order to tie to your message title (e.g., ranked high to low or low to high) not just in random or alphabetical order.

When using graphs, be especially aware of overriding PowerPoint defaults that lead to "chartjunk," as explained on page 129.

EXAMPLES OF GRAPHS

To show . . .	Use a graph like this . . .
Parts of a whole • Components • Percentages • Shares	Pie 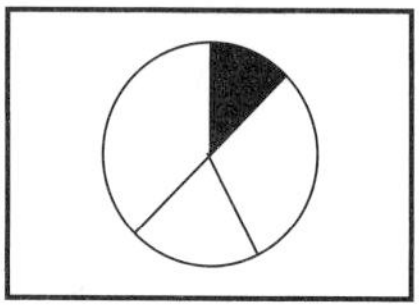 / Exploded Pie 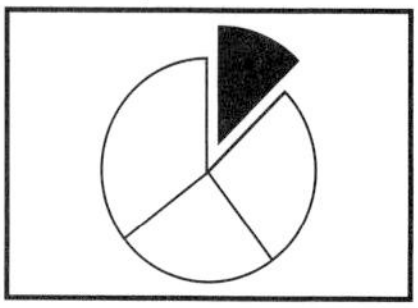
One item compared to others • Rank • More or less than • Difference among	Bar 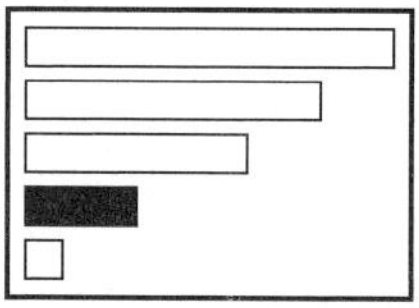 / Column 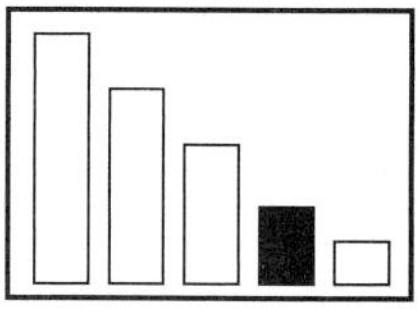
Components of multiple items • Percentages • Shares • Proportions	Subdivided Bar  / Subdivided Column 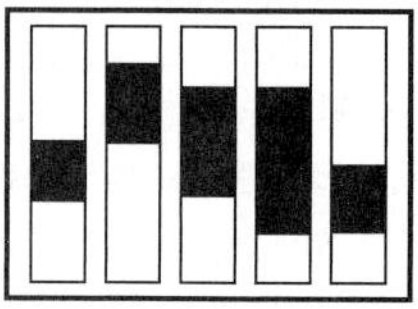
Changes over time or frequency • Increase/decrease • Concentrations • Trends	Line 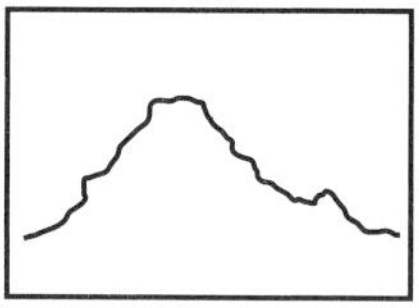 / Column 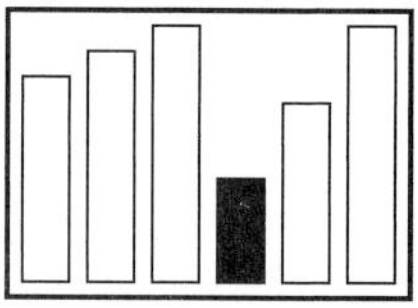
Correlation • Relation • Pattern • Deviation from pattern	Scatter 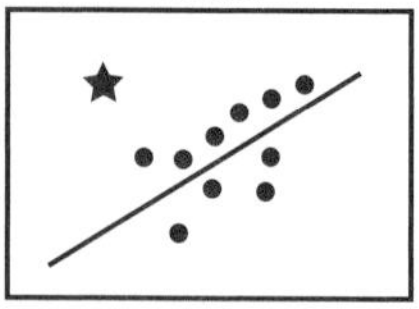 / Paired Bar 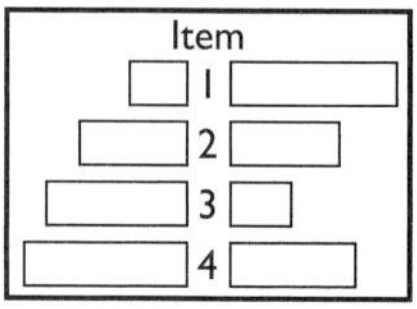 (Item 1, 2, 3, 4)

Adapted from G. Zelazny

LABELING GRAPHS

**1. Preferred option:
Label inside section**

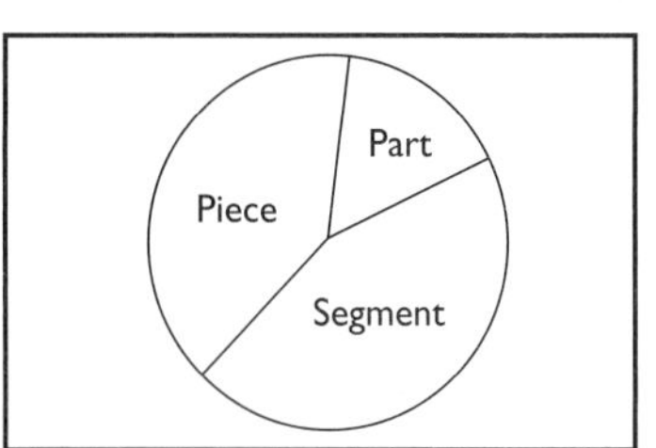

**2. Second-best option:
Label just outside section**

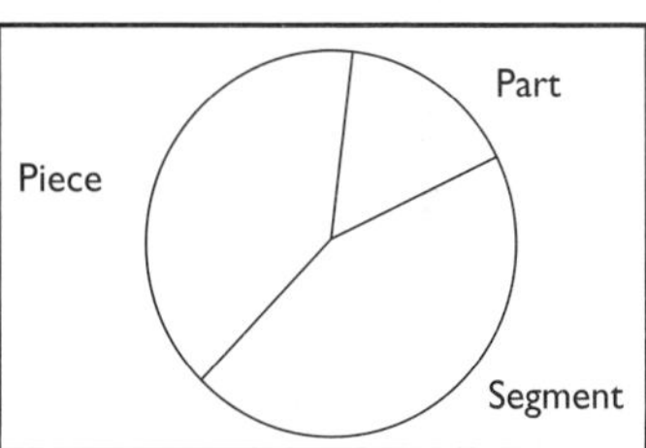

**3. Third-best option:
Label and connect to section with line**

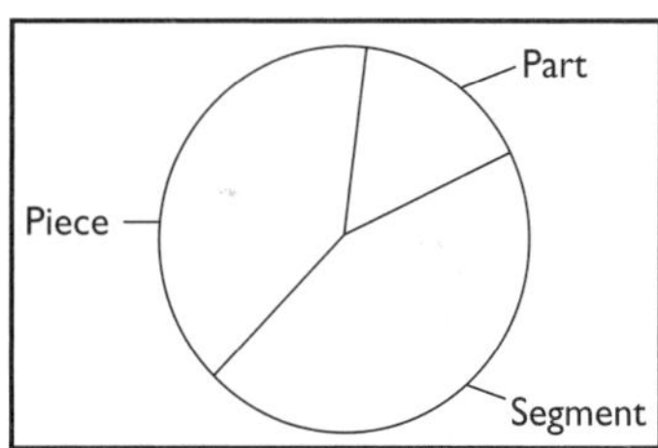

**4. Worst option:
Use a legend**

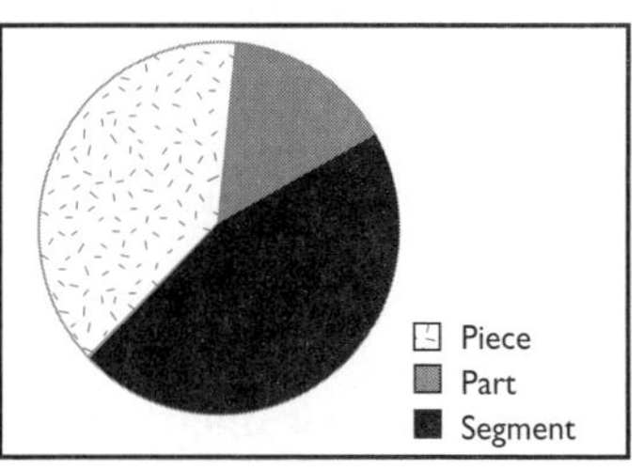

3. Designing concept diagrams to show "how"

In addition to showing quantitative data visually on graphs, think about ways in which you can show nonquantitative relationships visually on diagrams—especially to add excitement to your visuals and to reach the 40% of your audience who are probably visual learners. For example, compare the following two agendas.

Agenda as word slide

Input three sets of data to price our new product

- Company costs
- Economic value to customer
- Competitive prices

Agenda as concept diagram

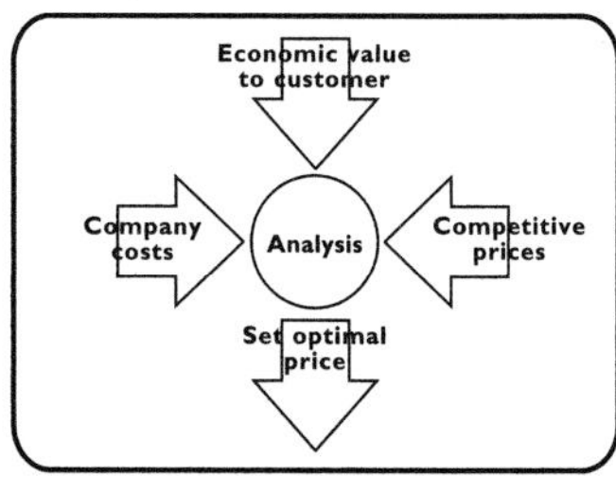

Use concept diagrams to show relationships visually. As visuals expert Edward Tufte points out in his diatribe against "death by bullet list," the relationship among the three points is unclear in the following bullet list:

Bullet list: relationship among points unclear

- Increase market share
- Increase profits
- Increase number of new products

In contrast, the following concept diagrams show three possible relationships among the same three points:

Concept diagrams: relationships are clear

Market share → Profits → New products

New products → Market share; New products → Profits

Profits → New products → Market share

Make sure concept diagrams make sense visually. Concept diagrams must be based on a viaual concept. For example, don't use arrows unless one idea actually leads to the next; don't use an overlap diagram unless the concepts actually overlap; place ideas of equal importance on the same level; group similar ideas together visually.

The table below provides some examples of concept diagrams. For many more such examples, see *Say It With Charts* or *Tools for Facilitating Team Meetings,* both listed in the bibliography.

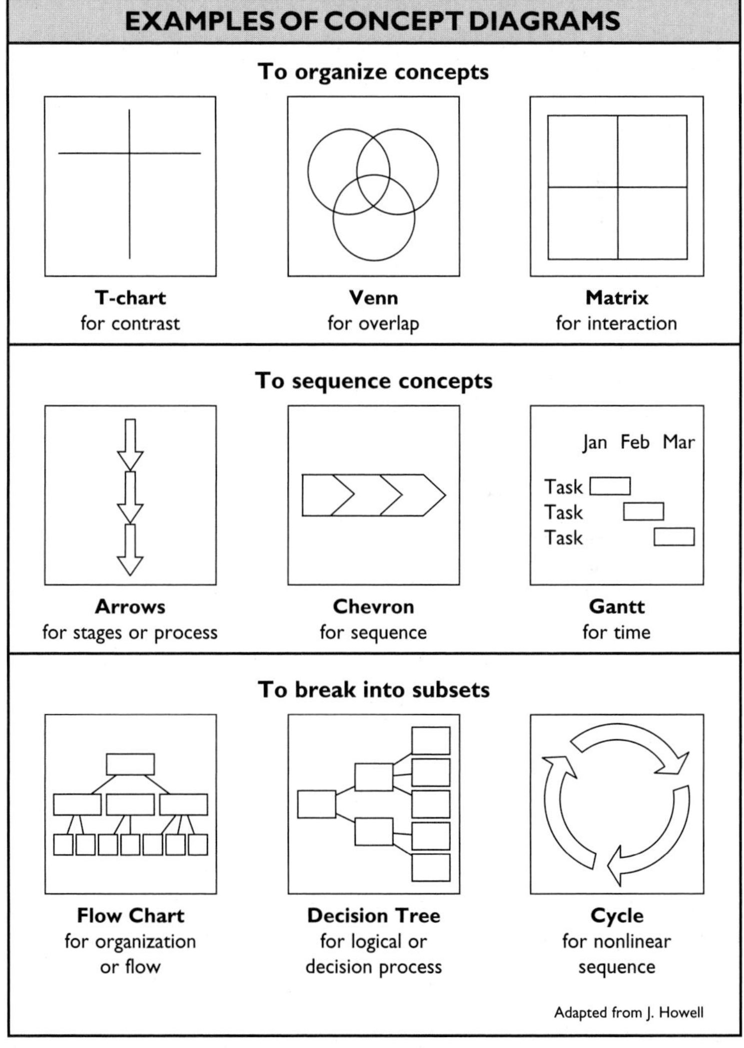

4. Designing word charts to show "why" or "how"

Virtually all business presentations include word charts to reinforce the main ideas and structure of the presentation. When using word charts, however, keep in mind the following guidelines.

Use stand-alone sense. Just like your message titles, the text of your word charts should make comprehensible stand-alone sense to (1) someone seeing it for the first time, (2) latecomers, or (3) someone reading your slides later.

Ineffective bullet text: Lacks stand-alone sense	*Effective bullet text: Makes stand-alone sense*
• Product	• Unique business model
• Market analysis	• Large market with unmet needs
• Competition	• No direct competition
• Operations	• Institute six-step process

Remember the "six by six" guideline. As a general rule of thumb, keep in mind the guideline proposed by presentation expert Lynn Russell: think "six by six"—a maximum of six lines per word chart and an average of six words per line. If you have more than two lines of text in a bullet, either simplify the wording or break it into a main heading plus subpoints. Obviously, it may be appropriate to break this guideline if necessary, but do not do so on slide after slide—and turn your presentation into a group reading session.

Use telegram language. Pare down your word charts to include key words and phrases only. Use what presentation expert Charlotte Rosen calls "telegram language"—that is, sentences or phrases minus most articles, auxiliary verbs, and prepositions.

Ineffective: does not use telegram language

XYZ Corporation has been downgraded by Moody's.

ABC has continued the push for globalization of purchasing.

Effective: uses telegram language

Moody's downgrades XYZ.

ABC continues to push for globalized purchasing.

Don't use word charts as scripts. Don't think of your word charts as word-for-word scripts that echo what you are saying throughout the presentation. Instead, reserve word charts for points you really want to emphasize. The following two examples show the agenda for the same presentation: the first in complete sentences, as a word-for-word script; the second edited down to key phrases only.

Ineffective: word-for-word script

INTRODUCTION

Over the past two decades, the waste management industry has undertaken planning as a response to growing markets and an increasingly competitive environment. Understanding historical environmental trends and how they are expected to change is critical to the development of successful strategies of Boford Industries. The purpose of this presentation is to

- Examine the waste management industry today and how it got there
- Assess future trends and their implications
- Discuss how other companies are reacting and changing in response to the external environment

Effective: key ideas only

Presentation Agenda
Boford Industries

- Examine historical trends
- Assess future trends
- Analyze competition

Don't misuse bullet lists. (1) Use bullets for sequence (first to last), priority (most to least, or vice versa), or membership in a set. For any other relationship among your points, use a concept diagram instead. (2) Don't use bullets unless you have at least two items listed.

Use indentation effectively. Indent the entire bullet section, as illustrated here.

Ineffective indentation

• Here is a bad example of bullet indentation in which the bullet does not stand out very much because the subsequent lines "wrap around" it.

• Here is another bad example of bullet indentation in which the bullet does not stand out very much either—this time because only the first line is indented.

Effective indentation

- Here is a good example of bullet indentation. All of the lines are indented equally, so the bullet point itself "stands out" on its own. For effective bullet indentation, use the "hanging indent" feature on your software program.

Check your line breaks. Try to avoid having one word all alone on a line, especially in titles.

Ineffective line break: one word alone on a line

> Combination increases value-added products and
> services

Effective line break

> Combination increases value-added
> products and services

Check for errors. Do not undercut your credibility with grammatical or spelling errors on your slides. These kinds of errors are more noticeable and glaring on a large screen in front of a group of people than they are in a printed document. In particular, check for both grammatical and conceptual parallelism, as explained on page 54.

5. Editing each slide

Microedit your visuals just as you would microedit your writing. In addition to editing wordiness (as explained on the preceding two pages), cut overload and extraneous graphics.

Avoid overload. Avoid overloaded text or graphic visuals that include too much complexity for one chart. Audience members may end up reading and pondering these charts instead of listening to you; at worst, they may get completely lost. Therefore, for each visual, decide what is most important for the audience to see. If you find yourself with an overloaded visual, such as the one shown in the examples that follow, you might choose to either (1) simplify it so that the key ideas, figures, or trends are emphasized, as illustrated in the bottom of the figure, or (2) cut it so that one section is shown in detail, or (3) break it into a series of overlays or progressive "builds," each of which shows an added layer of detail.

Examples: overloaded and simplified

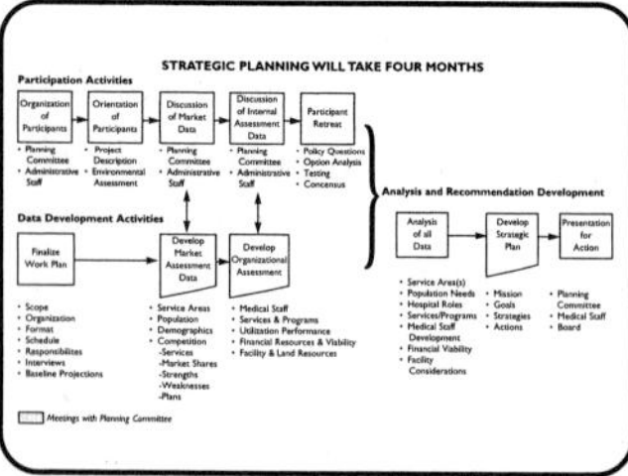

Delete chartjunk. To use the term invented by visual design expert Edward Tufte, delete "chartjunk"—that is, any extraneous design elements that do not contribute to your message. Regain control of your slides by modifying the chartjunk temptations inherent in PowerPoint.

- *Get rid of all legends* (as shown below) that slow down your viewers; instead, insert labels manually on or near the bars, slices of pie, and so on (as shown on page 123).
- *Use 2D, not 3D:* To avoid misleading your viewers, always choose two-dimensional, rather than three-dimensional, views in graphs.
- *Increase boldness of trend lines* to make them readable.
- *Modify width and spacing:* Modify chart elements to make skinny bars and columns wider and decrease the space between them. In general, the space between each of them should be less than their width.
- *Modify automatic color* choices to eliminate "fruit salad" (see page 115) and ensure use of only your chosen accent color (as explained on pages 115 and 120).
- *Ban visual invasions* like ready-made templates, invasive backgrounds, and distracting animations, as discussed on pages 114–117.
- *Limit use of Clip Art* such as head-scratching Screen Beans.
- *Change defaults* to eliminate any items that do not add any informational meaning—including gridlines, tick marks, cross-hatching, unnecessary shading or borders, and unnecessary decorations.

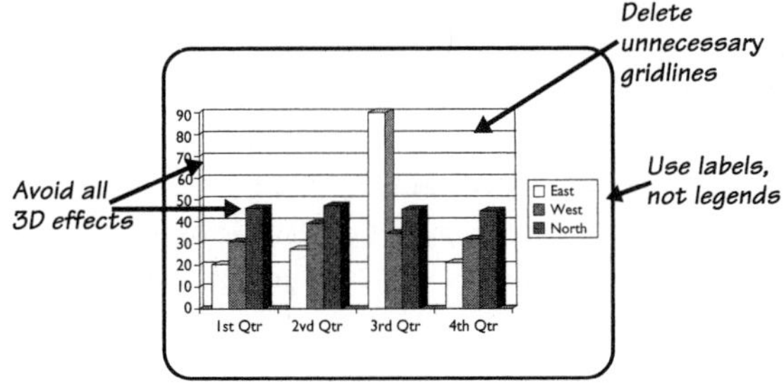

III. CHOOSING VISUAL AID EQUIPMENT

VISUAL AIDS			
I. Designing the presentation as a whole	II. Designing each individual slide	III. Choosing visual aid equipment	IV. Practicing with visual aids

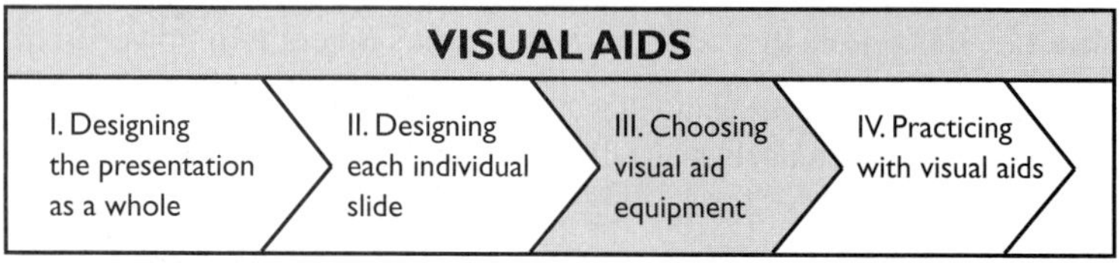

Base your equipment choice on your audience analysis, not just on what equipment you enjoy using most.

Analyze your audience first.

- *Audience expectations:* Find out whether any audience, organizational, or cultural expectations might influence which equipment to use.
- *Audience size:* Consider the size of the audience. For example, a whiteboard might work well for a group of 10, but it would be unreadable for a group of 80.
- *Audience formality:* You might choose to use a large-screen projector for a more formal group and a flipchart for a less formal one.
- *Audience participation:* Choose a deck or board for increased participation, a computer or overhead projector for less participation. (See pages 6–7 regarding tell/sell versus consult/join.)
- *Audience need for a permanent record:* Avoid using the whiteboard if they need a permanent record.

Then, choose your equipment. Although dozens of kinds of visual equipment are available (including electronic copy boards, document cameras, 35 mm slides, video, and film), by far the most prevalent in business today are (1) large-screen computer projectors, (2) decks or handouts, (3) whiteboards or flipcharts, and (4) overhead projectors. The advantages and disadvantages of each are described on the facing page. Practice techniques for each of them are covered in the rest of this chapter.

VISUAL AIDS EQUIPMENT	
Advantages	**Disadvantages**
Large-screen computer projectors	
• Can use multiple media (images, sounds, video, etc.) • Have animation ("build") function • Can provide printed hard copy • Can be sophisticated, dramatic, and even dazzling	• Are prone to technical problems • Usually need darkened room • Intimidate group discussion • Can't be changed real-time
Decks and handouts	
• Allow for bright room; more interactive than computer; allow everyone to sit • Show complex, detailed information • Can be used for audience note-taking and discussion • Provide hard copy: can be distributed before, during, or after the discussion	• Allow audience to read ahead and become distracted from what you are saying • Tend to become overloaded: too many and too complex
Whiteboards and flipcharts	
• Allow for bright room; good for discussion; can annotate real-time; low tech • *Boards:* unintimidating; good for spontaneity • *Flipcharts:* can attach to walls, provide permanent record	• Too small for large group; cannot show complex images • *Boards:* must erase for more space, no permanent record • *Flipcharts:* large and clumsy to transport
Overhead projectors	
• Portable, less complex, easy to use • Can annotate real-time • Allow random access to any slide	• May appear outdated • May block audience's view • Need somewhat darkened room • Lack animation ("build")

IV. PRACTICING WITH VISUAL AIDS

VISUAL AIDS			
I. Designing the presentation as a whole	II. Designing each individual slide	III. Choosing visual aid equipment	IV. Practicing with visual aids

All your work designing visual aids will be wasted if you don't use them effectively during your presentation. The following sections cover preparation techniques to integrate your visuals gracefully, unobtrusively, and effectively as you speak.

1. General preparation techniques

Here are six general practice suggestions for using your visuals effectively.

Familiarize yourself with the equipment. Become extremely comfortable with whatever equipment you have decided to use. Practice is especially important with high-tech visuals, visuals you haven't used much before, or visuals to be used in a new location or country.

- *Rehearse.* Don't lose credibility by fumbling with your visuals. Instead, practice repeatedly, especially with high-tech options. Practice by interacting with the equipment: actually set it up, turn it on, press the buttons, click the remote, insert the video, flip the pages, position the slides, and so on. Remember that each model of equipment has different quirks, from placement of the power switch to availability of spare bulbs.
- *Prepare a backup plan.* Think also about what you'll do if your equipment fails. Practice with your backup medium and prepare a time control chart in case visual aid trouble eats into your delivery time.

Introduce each visual. Visuals do not speak for themselves; it's your job to help them communicate your message.

- *State your oral transition before displaying the new slide.* Before you move to the next slide, state your backward look/forward look transition (as described on page 90) while you are displaying either your old slide or your repeated agenda slide (as described on page 112).
- *Then, display and explain the new slide.* Display the new slide, give your audience a few moments to take it in, then state the main idea of the new slide. To continue with the previous example, you might say, "As you can see, the Southwest division reached its $6 million goal."
- *Give the audience time.* Be sure to give the audience enough time to comprehend what you've said and to connect with each visual. Remember your audience has never seen your visuals before; therefore, it will take them longer to grasp the meaning of each visual than it will take you. Remember especially to slow down and use build for the agenda.
- *Explain complex visuals.* When showing complex visuals, introduce the main idea and then explain the meanings of colors, axes, or any symbols you've used. When possible, build complex charts and diagrams (as discussed on page 117) so you can provide this kind of explanation as you build the visual.

Cue the audience. Don't assume the audience knows where they are supposed to look. Tell them. Show them. Or do both.

- *Cues for PowerPoint:* One of the advantages of using PowerPoint is the variety of cueing options you have available. For example, you can build each bullet point or each part of a complex graph. Or, you can use bold arrows, boxes, or contrasting colors to cue the audience to look at a particular place on the screen.
- *Cues for decks:* One of the disadvantages of a deck presentation is that your audience can read whatever they want whenever they want. Try to keep them with you by (1) continually referring to page numbers (e.g., "As you can see on page 12") and (2) explaining use of color, axes, symbols, and so on, since you can't use build (e.g., "Note the hiring trend for consulting firms, shown as a blue line.")

Cues for pointing Pointing provides an effective way to use your hands and to keep audience's eyes focused where you want them.

- *Back up to the screen to point:* Avoid pointing vaguely in the general vicinity of the screen. Instead, if possible, back up to the screen and point right on the screen itself to the exact spot where you want the audience to focus. On the overhead, avoid pointing on the projector itself because any nervous shaking will be magnified on screen.
- *Stand to the left for bullet lists:* When using lots of bullet lists, try to stand to the left of the screen or flipchart, so you can point to the beginning of each line, rather than the end of it.
- *Use the arm closer to the screen:* Be sure to point with the "inside arm"—that is, the arm closer to the screen—instead of reaching across your body with the "outside arm" thereby turning your back to the audience.
- *Use your hand, not a pointer:* In general, use your hand and not a pointer. Most people who have a pointer in their hands cannot resist fiddling with it—extending it in and out, turning it, banging it against the defenseless screen, conducting with it, and so on. If you absolutely must use a pointer because you cannot reach the screen, then put it down when you are not using it.
- *Avoid laser pointers:* Laser pointers are even worse than others. The small red laser dot on a PowerPoint screen is virtually unreadable and if your hand is the least bit shaky, the dot appears to bounce around the screen.

Don't let your visuals distract the audience.

- *Get rid of "old news."* Once you are done with an image, transition to a blank screen, turn over the flipchart, or check with the audience and then erase the board. Don't talk about a new idea while showing an old visual.
- *Avoid empty white screens.* Big, empty, white screens are also distracting. Therefore, use the "blank screen" button or insert plain black slides into a slide show, or turn the overhead projector off if the blank screen would be showing for a long time.
- *Use "revealing lines" technique with caution.* When using an overhead projector, if you move a piece of paper or cardboard down the transparency to reveal one line at a time, it may drive some audience members absolutely crazy. For some reason, these same people don't seem to mind if you parcel out information by building text visuals in PowerPoint.

Make eye contact with your audience, not your visuals. Eye contact links you to the audience: they like it, because they feel more connected to you; you need to make it, so you can read their reactions to your presentation.

- *Don't be magnetized by your visuals.* A common problem with using visuals is that they become "eye-contact magnets"; presenters can't seem to stop looking at them. Therefore, be sure you only glance at your visuals and look at the audience as much as possible.
- *Be careful when writing.* Writing on flipcharts and whiteboards is especially challenging for maintaining eye contact.

  In most tell/ sell presentations, you should stop talking, write, then look at the audience and discuss what you've written.

  In interactive situations, you may have to write while someone else is speaking, but try to (1) look at the speaker as long as possible before breaking the connection and to look back afterward to confirm you got it right, or (2) use a scribe, as described on pages 99 and 137.
- *Glance at the screen only briefly.* When a new slide appears, it's fine to glance at the screen briefly (and take in the new slide at the same time your audience is doing so). But then, turn right back around to face the audience. If you do choose to glance back, do so by looking at the screen, where your audience is looking—never at the monitor, which your audience can't see. Including reduced copies of your slides on your notecards (as described on page 92) will also decrease your dependency on looking at the screen.

2. Techniques for specific equipment

In addition to the general advice about visual aids interaction provided in the previous section, here are a few ideas about how to meet the special challenges offered by the different kinds of equipment.

PowerPoint slide shows

- *Arrive very early*, especially if using unfamiliar equipment. Arrange to have someone help you if you haven't used the equipment before. Set up and test equipment as soon as possible.
- *Check the colors* on the large screen and modify if needed. What you see on your computer screen will not be the same as what you see on the large screen.
- *Practice with remote.* Handle it, practice clicking it unobtrusively, point it (only if necessary)—until you can use it without thinking.
- *Get rid of screen savers* if projecting from your laptop.

Decks and handouts

- *Assume people will read* whatever is in front of them. Therefore, try to control when to distribute hard copy: (1) *In advance:* general handouts (such as the agenda), handouts intended for note-taking, or decks intended to be read in advance. (2) *When you are discussing:* complex information or detailed handouts only at the exact time when you are discussing them. (3) *At the end:* detailed summaries or leave-behinds.
- *Maintain eye contact* and other nonverbal connection with the audience to encourage them not to lag behind or jump ahead in the deck. This advice is especially important if the culture or company dictates the use of decks, regardless of need.
- *Explain the deck's purpose* and how you will be using it as you speak.
- *Cue people* by referring to the page numbers on the deck.
- *Don't read* the deck. Talk to the audience, not the paper. If possible, put the deck on a table so you can gesture, and be sure to look up so you can make eye contact.
- *Remember that wire-bound decks* are easier to flip than those that are taped or stapled.

Overheads

- *Check your equipment.* Know where the spare bulb is and how to install it, or arrange for a backup projector. Be sure you have the right kind of marking pens—not flipchart markers or regular pens.
- *Make sure everyone can see the screen.* (1) Check to see if the projector or projector arm is blocking anybody's view. (2) Then, avoid standing next to the projector where you may also block someone's view; instead, stand back flush with the screen, so you can cue the audience by pointing on it. (3) Finally, don't walk between the screen and the projector when the projector is turned on.
- *Frame your overheads* so they are easier to handle and block the extra light; unframed overheads stick together and are harder to place evenly on the projector. Put a piece of masking tape across the bottom of the projector's screen to line up your overheads.

Flipcharts

- *Use thick markers* and highly visible colors (e.g., black, blue, and green; not orange or yellow). Keep spare markers nearby.
- *Write up the message titles* in advance to save time during the presentation.
- *Practice flipping pages* over when you are done with them.
- *Leave a blank page* between used pages. Turn pages by turning up the bottom corner and noting the page topic in pencil so you can easily find it and flip it when needed.
- *Bring masking tape* if you want to post pages around the room.
- *Practice with your scribe.* If you choose to work with a scribe (as discussed on page 99), make it clear in advance how you will work together. For example, tell the scribe to write only the words you signal him or her to write, or else tell the scribe to write at his or her discretion.

Besides your visual aids (covered in this chapter), think about your presentation structure (Chapter V) and nonverbal delivery (Chapter VII). The checklist on page 156 summarizes all three of these sets of speaking skills.

CHAPTER VII OUTLINE

I. Nonverbal delivery skills
   1. Body language
   2. Vocal qualities
   3. Space and objects
   4. Practice and arrangements
   5. Physical relaxation
   6. Mental relaxation
   7. Last-minute relaxation

II. Nonverbal listening skills
   1. Attending skills
   2. Encouraging skills
   3. Following skills

CHAPTER VII

Speaking: Nonverbal Skills

Your words (Chapter V) and your visual aids (Chapter VI) make up only a portion of what you communicate. In fact, experts estimate that 60% to 90% of what you communicate is nonverbal. This chapter covers those nonverbal messages you send—the way you appear and sound to others.

The first part of the chapter covers nonverbal delivery skills to use in tell/sell presentations. The second part concentrates on the nonverbal listening skills to use in various consult/join interactive situations. The examples in this chapter are based on Anglo-American business practices; keep in mind that nonverbal communication varies widely across different cultures, as discussed on pages 29–31.

NONVERBAL SKILLS		
Section in this chapter:	**I. Nonverbal Delivery Skills**	**II. Nonverbal Listening Skills**
Who speaks most:	You	Your audience
Purposes:	To inform or to persuade	To understand
Typical situations:	Tell/sell presentations	Questions and answers Consult/join meetings One-to-one conversations

I. NONVERBAL DELIVERY SKILLS

NONVERBAL SKILLS		
Section in this chapter:	**I. Nonverbal Delivery Skills**	**II. Nonverbal Listening Skills**
Who speaks most:	You	Your audience
Purposes:	To inform or to persuade	To understand
Typical situations:	Tell/sell presentations	Questions and answers Consult/join meetings One-to-one conversations

Nonverbal delivery skills include body language, vocal qualities, and space and objects around you.

1. Body language

Keep in mind these five elements of body language.

Posture Effective speakers exhibit poise through their posture.

- Stand in a relaxed, professional manner—comfortably upright, squarely facing your audience, with your weight balanced and distributed evenly. Your feet should be aligned under your shoulders—neither too close nor too far apart.
- Watch out for (1) rocking, swaying, or bouncing; (2) leaning, slouching, or the "hip sit"; (3) "frozen" poses such as the stiff "Attention!" or the wide-legged "cowpoke straddle" stances.

Body movement Body movement varies by personality and room size.

- Move naturally. You don't have to stand stock-still or to plan every move. Examples of effective body movement include leaning forward to emphasize a point or walking back to point to the screen.
- Avoid random, nervous, quick, or constant movements.

Hand and arm gestures Effective speakers use their hands the same way they would conversationally; in addition, they use them to point on screen, as explained on pages 132–137.

- Let your hands do whatever they would be doing if you were speaking to one person instead of to a group. Be yourself: some people use expansive gestures; others are more reserved. For example, use them to move conversationally, to be still for a while, to emphasize a point, to describe an object, or to point to a particular line on your visual aid.
- Avoid putting your hands in any one position and leaving them there without change—such as the "figleaf" (hands clasped in front), the "parade rest" (hands clasped in back), the "gunshot wound" (hand clutching opposite arm), or the "podium clutch." Avoid nervous-looking gestures, such as ear-tugging or arm-scratching. Finally, avoid "authority killers" like flipping your hair or waving your arms randomly.

Facial expression Your facial expression should also look natural, as it would in conversation.

- Keep your face relaxed to look interested and animated. Vary your expression according to the subject and the occasion.
- Avoid a stony, deadpan expression; also, avoid inappropriate facial expression, such as smiling when you are talking about something sad or negative.

Eye contact Eye contact is a crucial nonverbal skill. It makes possible what communication expert Lynn Russell calls the "listener/speaker connection"—the audience feels connected with you and you feel connected with them and can read their reactions.

- *Do look:* Look throughout the entire room, establishing momentary (that is, about two-second) contact with individuals in your audience. You might try, for starters, looking at the friendly faces; their nodding and smiling will encourage you. Eventually, however, you should look at everyone—especially the key decision makers in the group. You don't need to keep 100% eye contact; you may need to look away briefly to think. If, after your presentation, you can remember what the people in your audience looked like, you had good eye contact.
- *Avoid looking:* Avoid looking constantly at a manuscript or notecards, at the visual aids or screen, at the middle of the back of the room, at the ceiling, or at the floor. Don't show a preference for looking at one side of the room or the other. Finally, avoid fake eye contact—such as "eye dart," eyes moving back and forth very rapidly, or the back-and-forth "lighthouse scan."

2. Vocal qualities

Many people underestimate the importance of the voice in establishing credibility. See page 147 for vocal relaxation exercises.

Inflection and volume The term *inflection* refers to variation in your pitch, which creates an expressive, nonmonotonous sound; *volume* refers to how loudly you speak.

- Speak with expressiveness and enthusiasm, in a warm, pleasant tone, with pitch variety. Use volume appropriate for the size of the room. Breathe deeply and fully.
- Avoid the common problem of speaking in a dull, robotic monotone that sounds as if you are bored. Do not speak too quietly to be heard or too loudly for the size of the room. Also, watch out for a tendency to end declarative sentences as if they were questions.

Rate Rate is the speed at which you speak.

- Vary your rate somewhat to avoid droning. Generally, keep it slow enough to be understood but fast enough to maintain energy. Use pauses, or "mental punctuation," before or after a key term, to separate items in a series, or to indicate a major break in thought.
- Watch out for speaking at a monotonous, constant rate. An ineffective rate lacks pauses or variation: if too slow, it may bore your audience; if too fast, it may lose them.

Fillers Fillers are verbal pauses—like *uh*, *er*, *um*, and *ya know*.

- Pause during your presentation to collect your thoughts. You don't need to fill the pause with a filler.
- Don't overreact if you notice a few fillers; everybody uses them occasionally. If you diagnose a distracting, habitual, overuse of fillers, however, try asking a colleague to signal you every time you use one.

Enunciation Enunciation is the clarity of your articulation.

- Pronounce your words clearly and crisply—without mumbling, running words together, leaving out syllables, or dropping final consonants.
- Avoid mumbling, which may be perceived as sounding uneducated or hurried. Avoid running words together—as in *gonna* or *wanna*—which is often associated with talking too fast. Avoid leaving out syllables, as in *guvmint*. Finally, avoid dropping final consonants, as in *thousan'*, *jus'*, or *goin'*.

3. Space and objects

Another component of nonverbal communication is the use of space and objects around you. Objects and space affect four sets of choices: seating arrangements, speaker height and distance, use of objects, and dress.

Seating The way you arrange the chairs for a presentation will communicate nonverbally what kind of interaction you want to have with your audience. Choose straight lines of chairs for the least interactive sessions. Choose horseshoe-shaped or u-shaped lines of chairs to encourage more interaction. For smaller groups, choose either (1) a rectangular table, with a person seated at the head, to emphasize the power of the leader, or (2) a round table to encourage equality among participants.

Height and distance The higher you are in relation to your audience, the more formal the atmosphere you are establishing nonverbally. Therefore, the most formal presentations might be delivered from a stage or a platform. In a semiformal situation, you stand while your audience sits. To make the situation even less formal, place yourself and your audience at the same level: sit together around a table or seat yourself in front of the group. Similarly, the closer you are, the less formal you appear.

Objects The more objects you place between yourself and the audience, the more formal the interaction. To increase formality, use a podium, desk, or table between yourself and the audience. To decrease formality, stand or sit without any articles of furniture between you and your audience.

Dress What you wear also communicates something to your audience. Dress to project the image that you want to create. Dress appropriately for the audience, the occasion, the organization, and the culture. For instance, what is appropriate in the fashion industry may be totally inappropriate in the banking industry. Finally, don't wear clothes that will distract from what you are saying—such as exaggerated, dangling jewelry or a loud, flashy tie.

4. Practice and arrangements

Using the following practice and arrangement techniques will improve your nonverbal delivery.

Practice techniques Here are some possible practice techniques.

- *Avoid reading or memorizing.* You won't be able to establish eye contact or rapport if you are reading; you won't have time to memorize every presentation. Instead, practice speaking conversationally, referring to your notecards as necessary.
- *Rehearse out loud on your feet.* Knowing your content and saying it aloud are two completely different activities, so do not practice by sitting and reading over your notecards. Instead, practice out loud and on your feet. For an important presentation, rehearse the entire thing out loud and on your feet. For a less important presentation, practice the opening, closing, and main transitions this way.
- *Memorize three key parts.* Another suggestion is to memorize your opening, closing, and major transitions. These are the times when speakers feel the most nervous and are most apt to lose composure.
- *Practice with your visuals.* As we discussed on pages 132–137, become familiar with your equipment; make sure it works and you know how to use it smoothly. Practice to integrate what you are saying with what you are showing and to avoid delivery problems such as talking to the screen or aggressively thrusting the remote toward the screen.
- *Improve your delivery.* While you're practicing, you can work to improve your delivery by videotaping your rehearsal, by practicing in front of a friend or a colleague, or by speaking into a mirror to improve your facial expression or an audiotape recorder to improve your vocal expression.
- *Simulate the situation.* You might try practicing in the actual place where you will be making the presentation or in front of chairs set up as they will be when you speak.
- *Time yourself.* Time yourself in advance to avoid the irritating problem of running overtime during your presentation. You prefer a short presentation; so does your audience. During your rehearsal, remember to (1) speak slowly, as you would to actual people, rather than just reading through your ideas; (2) speak extra slowly during your preview, to give the audience enough time to digest it; (3) include time to change and explain your slides; (4) add some time for interruptions and questions; and then (5) add in some extra time because the real presentation usually takes 10 to 20% longer than the practice version.

Arrangement reminders In addition to practicing, another way to gain confidence is to make the necessary arrangements for your presentation so that you won't be flustered upon discovering your computer doesn't work or you have too few chairs. All the work you do to create a presentation may be wasted if you haven't made such arrangements. Remember that you are responsible for your own arrangements. Although the janitor, your secretary, or the audiovisual technician can help you out, you are the one who will be suffering in front of the audience if arrangements go awry.

You will deliver your presentation more effectively if you do not arrive at the last moment. Get there about 30 minutes early to check the arrangements, fix anything that may be wrong, get comfortable with the place, and mingle with the audience.

- *Room:* First, double-check your room arrangements. Make sure that you have enough chairs, but not too many. Get rid of extras in advance; people don't like to move once they're seated. Make sure that the chairs are arranged as you want them and that any other items you ordered are there and functioning. Check the lighting, ventilation, sources of noise, and any other potential distractions. (If, despite your best efforts, a distraction occurs during the presentation, don't get flustered or pretend it's not happening. Deal with it as naturally as you can.)
- *Visual aids:* Second, check your visual aid arrangements. Make sure that all the equipment and accessories you ordered have arrived. Test all the equipment far enough in advance so that you can get someone to fix or replace it if necessary. Get the number to call if something should break down during your presentation. Test the readability of your slides or handwriting by viewing them from the farthest chair or asking someone seated in the back row. Make sure that every person in the audience will be able to see your visuals. Finally, check the sequence of your slides and handouts.
- *Yourself:* Finally, arrange yourself (as it were). Set up your notecards and anything else you might need, such as a glass of water. Remember that you are "on stage" from the moment the first person arrives. Prepare yourself physically and mentally by using one of the specific relaxation techniques described on the following six pages.

5. Physical relaxation

When speaking in front of a group, most people feel a surge of adrenaline. In fact, fear of public speaking ranks as Americans' number-one fear—ahead of both death and loneliness. Most people experience this burst of adrenaline. The trick, however, is to get that energy working for you, instead of working against you, by finding an effective relaxation technique. Experiment with the various methods explained on the next six pages until you find the one or two techniques that are most useful for you.

The first set of relaxation techniques is based on the assumption, shared by many performers and athletes, that by relaxing yourself physically, you will calm yourself mentally.

Exercise One way to relax is to exercise before a presentation. Many people calm down following the physical exertion of running, working out, or other athletic activities.

Progressive relaxation Developed by psychologist Edmund Jacobson, this technique involves tensing and relaxing muscle groups. To practice this technique, set aside about 10 to 15 minutes of undisturbed time in a comfortable, darkened place where you can lie down. Tense (by clenching vigorously for five to seven seconds) and relax (by releasing and enjoying the feeling for at least 10 seconds) each muscle group in turn: face, neck and chest, arms and hands, chest and upper back, stomach and lower back, upper legs, lower legs, and feet. Repeat the procedure at least twice.

Deep breathing For at least one full minute, sit or lie on your back with your hand on your diaphragm, just below the rib cage.

- *Yoga "sigh breath":* Inhale slowly through your nose to the count of four, feeling your diaphragm expand. Exhale even more slowly through your mouth feeling your diaphragm empty—to the count of six to eight, or counting backwards from four—and sighing aloud.
- *Sarnoff squeeze:* Similarly, speech coach Dorothy Sarnoff recommends inhaling through your nose and exhaling through your mouth, making a "sssss" sound and contracting the abdominus rectus muscles, what she calls the "vital triangle" just below the rib cage.

Specific body parts For some people, stage fright manifests itself in certain parts of the body—for example, tensed shoulders, quivering arms, or fidgety hands. Here are some exercises to relax specific body parts.

- *Neck and throat:* Gently roll your neck from side to side, front to back, chin to chest, or all the way around.
- *Shoulders:* Raise one or both shoulders as if you were shrugging. Then roll them back, then down, then forward. After several repetitions, rotate in the opposite direction.
- *Arms:* Shake out your arms, first only at the shoulders, then only at the elbow, finally letting your hands flop at the wrist.
- *Hands:* Repeatedly clench and relax your fists. Start with an open hand and close each finger one by one to make a fist; hold the clench; then release.
- *Face:* Close your eyes and wiggle your face muscles: forehead, nose, cheeks, and jaws. Move your jaw side-to-side.

Vocal relaxation Some nervous symptoms affect your voice—such as quivering, dry mouth, or sounding out-of-breath. Here are some general suggestions for keeping your voice in shape:

- *Be awake and rested.* Get enough sleep the night before your presentation, so your voice will be rested. Wake up several hours before your presentation to provide a natural warm-up period for your voice.
- *Take a hot shower.* A hot shower will wake up your voice; the steam will soothe a tired or irritated set of vocal cords.
- *Drink warm liquids.* Ideal candidates are herbal tea and warm water with lemon. Warm liquids with caffeine are fine for your voice, but they might increase your heart rate.
- *Avoid consuming milk* or other dairy products. Dairy products tend to coat the vocal cords, which may cause problems during your presentation.
- *Avoid dry mouth* by sucking a cough drop or hard candy, chewing gum, or biting your tongue before the presentation.
- *Hum* to warm up your voice. Start slowly and quietly, gradually adding a full range of pitches.
- *During the presentation:* (1) *Drink water:* Keep water nearby. If you have dry mouth, pause and drink as needed. (2) *Breathe deeply* from the diaphragm (below the rib cage), not shallowly from the shoulders or upper chest.

6. Mental relaxation

Some speakers prefer mental relaxation techniques—to control physical sensation mentally. Here are various mental relaxation techniques to try until you find one that works for you.

Think positively. Base your thinking on the Dale Carnegie argument: To feel brave, act as if you are brave. To feel confident, act as if you are confident.

Repeat positive words or phrases. Fill your mind with positive words or phrases, such as "poised, perfect, prepared, poised, perfect, prepared."

Think nonjudgmentally. Describe your behavior ("I notice a monotone") rather than judging it ("I have a terrible speaking voice!"). Then change the behavior by thinking rationally or using a positive self-picture, both of which are described below.

Think rationally. Avoid becoming trapped in the "ABCs of emotional reactions," as developed by psychologist Albert Ellis. **A** stands for the "activating event" (such as catching yourself using a filler word), which sparks an irrational **B** or "belief system" (such as "I must be absolutely perfect in every way; if I'm not perfect, then I must be terrible"), which causes **C** or "consequences" (such as anxiety or depression). Ellis recommends **D** or "disputing" these ABCs with a rational thought (such as "I don't demand absolute perfection from other speakers" or "Using one filler word is not the end of the world. I'll go on naturally instead of getting flustered.")

Use a positive self-picture. Many speakers find that positive self-pictures work better than positive words.

- *Visualize yourself as successful.* Visualize yourself hearing positive comments or applause. Then act out the role of the person you visualized.
- *Use a positive video picture.* Using a video of yourself speaking, freeze the frame at a point where you look effective. During your next presentation, visualize, then recreate, that person.
- *Think of yourself as the guru.* Remind yourself that you know your subject matter.
- *Put yourself "in character"* of a good speaker by your comportment and dress.

Don't think. (1) *While you are waiting to speak,* fill your mind with something mindless, like saying the alphabet. (2) *While you are speaking,* turn off your internal self-analysis and don't think about how you look or sound.

Try visualization. Relax by conjuring up in your mind a visual image of a positive and pleasant object or scene.

- *Imagine a scene.* On each of the several days before the presentation, close your eyes and imagine a beautiful, calm scene, such as a beach you have visited. Imagine the details of temperature, color, and fragrance. If your mind wanders, bring it back to your scene. Concentrate on the image and exclude all else. Try repeating positive phrases, such as "I feel warm and relaxed" or "I feel content."
- *Juxtapose the stress.* A few days before the presentation, visualize the room, the people, and the stresses. Then distance yourself and relax by visualizing the pleasant image. This technique decreases stress by defusing the situation in your mind.

Connect with the audience. Try to see your audience as real people.

- *Meet them and greet them.* When people are arriving, greet them, get to know some of them. Then, when you're speaking, find those people in the audience and feel as if you're having a one-to-one conversation with them.
- *Remember they are individuals.* Even if you can't greet the people in the audience, think of them as individual people, not as an amorphous audience. As you speak, imagine you are conversing with them.
- *Imagine you are speaking to a friend,* not to a group.
- *"Befriend" the audience.* Picture yourself in your own home, enthusiastically talking with old friends. Try to maintain a sense of warmth and goodwill. This altered perception can not only diffuse your anxiety, but also increase your positive energy.

Transform negative to positive. Consider the adrenaline that may be causing nervous symptoms as a positive energy. All speakers may feel butterflies in their stomachs; effective speakers get those butterflies to fly in formation, thereby transforming negative into positive energy.

7. Last-minute relaxation

When it's actually time to deliver the presentation, here are a few relaxation techniques that you can use at the last minute—and even as you speak.

Last-minute physical relaxation Obviously, you cannot start doing push-ups or practice humming as you're sitting or standing there, about ready to begin speaking. Fortunately, however, there are some other techniques that you can use to relax your body at the last minute—techniques no one can see you using.

- *Isometric exercises:* Clench and then quickly relax your muscles. For example, you might press or wiggle your feet against the floor, one hand against your other hand, or your hands against the table or chair; you might clench your fists, thighs, or toes. Then quickly relax the muscles you just clenched.
- *Deep breathing exercises:* Inhale slowly and deeply from the diaphragm, then exhale slowly and completely. Pause between breaths. Try breathing in through your nose and out through your mouth. Or, try imagining you are breathing in "the good" and breathing out "the bad." Avoid hyperventilating or shallow breathing from your upper chest.

Last-minute mental relaxation Also at the last minute, you may dispel stage fright mentally by using what behavioral psychologists call "internal dialogue," which means, of course, talking to yourself. Here are some examples:

- *Give yourself a pep talk.* "What I am about to say is important" or "I am ready" or "They are just people."
- *Play up your audience's reception.* "They are interested in my topic" or "They are a friendly group of people."
- *Repeat positive phrases.* "I'm glad I'm here; I'm glad you're here" or "I know I know" or "I care about you."

As you speak Finally, here are four techniques that you can use to relax even as you speak.

- *Speak to the "motivational listeners."* There are always a few kind souls out there who nod, smile, and generally react favorably. Especially at the beginning of your presentation, look at them, not at the people reading, looking out the window, or yawning. Looking at positive listeners will increase your confidence. Soon you will be looking at the people around those good listeners and ultimately at every person in the audience.
- *Talk to someone in the back row.* At the beginning of the presentation, take a deep breath and talk to the person in the back row to force breathing and volume.
- *Remember that you probably look better than you think you do.* Your nervousness is probably not as apparent to your audience as it is to you. Experiments show that even trained speech instructors do not see all the nervous symptoms speakers think they are exhibiting. Managers and students watching videotapes of their performances regularly say, "Hey, I look better than I thought I would!"
- *Concentrate on the here and now.* Focus on your ideas and your audience. Forget about past regrets and future uncertainties. You have already analyzed what to do; now just do it wholeheartedly. Enjoy communicating your information to your audience, and let your enthusiasm show.

II. NONVERBAL LISTENING SKILLS

NONVERBAL SKILLS		
Section in this chapter:	**I. Nonverbal Delivery Skills**	**II. Nonverbal Listening Skills**
Who speaks most:	You	Your audience
Purposes:	To inform or to persuade	To understand
Typical situations:	Tell/sell presentations	Questions and answers Consult/join meetings One-to-one conversations

In the first part of this chapter, we looked at nonverbal delivery skills to use when delivering a presentation. In this second section, we will consider a second set of nonverbal skills: the nonverbal listening skills to use in interactive situations.

Various studies show that businesspeople spend 45% to 63% of their time listening, yet as much as 75% of what gets said is ignored, misunderstood, or forgotten. Why? In part, because most of us have had little or no training in listening; because we can think at least four times faster than someone can talk; and because sometimes it's hard to avoid jumping to conclusions or becoming defensive before we've heard the other person out.

By learning to listen well, you will not only receive and retain better information, but you will also be more persuasive, because you will satisfy your audience's desire to be heard and you will improve your rapport and your audience's morale.

The following framework for improving listening skills is adapted from listening expert Robert Bolton. The three listening skills clusters include (1) attending skills, (2) encouraging skills, and (3) following skills. (For more information on listening and one-to-one communication, see the *Guide to Interpersonal Communication,* cited on page 181.)

1. Attending skills

The term "attending skills" means giving physical attention to the speaker—"listening" with your body—either one-on-one or with a group. These techniques will, of course, vary in different cultures.

Posture of involvement To look involved, your posture should look relaxed, yet alert. Maintain an open position, with your arms uncrossed. Do not stay rigid or unmoving; move in response to what the speaker is saying. When seated, lean forward toward the speaker, facing him or her squarely. One technique to show interest nonverbally is to mirror the same degree of formality in your posture as the other person is using.

Eye contact Eye contact also signals interest and involvement. Maintain steady, comfortable eye contact for a few seconds, then gaze around the speaker's face to "read" his or her expression, then back to the eyes. Do not glance toward distant objects, which signals noninterest. Avoid such obvious signs of rudeness as looking at your watch or gazing out the window.

Distance Sit or stand at the appropriate distance from the speaker—neither too close nor too far apart. Cross-cultural expert Edward Hall has identified zones of space in Anglo-American culture: 18 inches to 4 feet is "personal space"; 0 to 18 inches is "intimate space." But perhaps the best way to judge distance is by awareness of the audience comfort level: if the other person is leaning away, you're too close; if leaning toward you, you may be too far away. When seated, remember that the head of the table is associated with dominance and that sitting beside someone may be perceived as cooperative, while sitting across from someone may be perceived as competitive. In one-to-one situations, avoid standing or sitting at a higher level than the other person.

Eliminating barriers To give your undivided attention, try to remove any possible distractions. In your office, for example, you might have your calls held, close your door, and come out from behind your desk. In a group situation, you might come out from behind a podium or table. In addition, remove any mental barriers: for example, don't think about other tasks, make plans, or daydream.

2. Encouraging skills

In addition to using nonverbal attending skills, use the following three "encouraging skills" to let the other person speak and to avoid speaking too much yourself.

Door openers "Door openers" are nonjudgmental, reassuring ways of inviting other people to speak if they want to. For example, "All right. Let's hear what the rest of you have to say about this" or "You look upset. Care to talk about it?" In contrast, typical door closers include the following:

- *Criticizing:* "You get all upset no matter what we do!"
- *Advising:* "I was upset when I first heard of this too, but all you have to keep in mind is . . ."
- *Overusing logic:* "I don't see what you have to look so upset about. These numbers speak for themselves . . ."
- *Reassuring:* "Don't worry; I'm sure you'll understand after you hear . . . "
- *Stage-hogging:* Responding to someone else's story by telling one of your own. Even if you are trying to show understanding, they will often feel one-upped.

Open-ended questions One of the main ways to get people to talk is to ask them good questions. The questions designed to elicit the most information from others are known as "open-ended questions"—that is, questions that cannot be easily answered with a "yes" or "no." For example, you are likely to get more extensive responses if you

Ask	**Instead of**
Tell me about the computer project.	Is the computer project going well?
What concerns you about the deadlines on this schedule?	Can you meet the deadlines on this schedule?
How shall we solve this problem?	Do you like my solution?

Attentive silence and attention Perhaps the hardest listening skill of all is simply to stop talking. Effective listeners must learn to be comfortable with appropriate silence. Silence gives the other person time to think and to set the pace. Hear the speaker out, even if the message is unwelcome. Instead of talking or interrupting, show your interest by nodding your head and using "minimal encouragers," such as "I see," "Yes," or "Uh-huh."

3. Following skills

Paraphrasing content Paraphrasing means restating the other person's ideas accurately and concisely. Using this skill will enable you to check the accuracy of what you think you have heard, encourage the other person to elaborate on what he or she has said, and show that you are listening. Listen for main ideas, patterns, and themes, and organize those main thoughts as you listen, rather than judging or evaluating first. Then restate a few key words or summarize the key thoughts or idea. For example, "So, it sounds as if you are making three suggestions . . ." then list them or "Seems as though your major concern here is . . ."

Paraphrasing feelings In addition to hearing what the person says, be sensitive to how she or he says it. Listen "between the lines." Be aware of the speaker's tone of voice, volume, facial expression, and body movement. Examples of paraphrased feelings include "You sound upset about the new policy" or "You seem discouraged about the way your team is getting along" or "Looks like you're pleased with those results."

Note-taking or recording You may wish to take notes as you listen to show you are really interested and planning to follow up. In one-to-one situations, explain why you are taking notes; limit yourself to very few notes, so you don't lose your sense of connection; and consider sharing the notes as a summary. Sometimes, however, note-taking may be inappropriate. Gauge the situation to determine whether taking notes will make the speaker feel policed or whether you will concentrate too much on writing. Sometimes showing your concern with full eye contact is more important than recording the facts.

In a group situation, however, it's usually helpful to record participant comments on a flipchart or board—as described on page 137.

See the checklists on the following pages for a summary of all the skills covered in the previous three chapters, those used for (1) tell/sell presentations (structure, visuals, and nonverbal delivery) and (2) consult/join meetings (what you say and nonverbal listening skills). For more detailed books on these two skills, see *Guide to Presentations* and *Guide to Meetings*, both cited on page 182.

TELL/SELL PRESENTATION CHECKLIST

1. Verbal structure: what you say

See Chapter V

1. *Presentation structure:* Was your presentation structured effectively: opening, preview, clear main points, closing?
2. *Notes:* Did you prepare an outline?
3. *Questions and answers:* Did you decide when and how to take questions, and answer difficult questions effectively?

2. Visual aids: what your audience sees

See Chapter VI

1. *Presentation as a whole:* Were your visuals well designed for the presentation as a whole with effective structure, connection, colors, typography, and animation?
2. *Each individual slide:* Was each individual slide well designed: message titles, graphs to show "how much," concept diagrams to show "how," word charts to show "why" or "how," and no overload or chartjunk?
3. *Equipment:* Did you choose the appropriate equipment from among computer projection systems, still projection systems, animated projection systems, boards and charts, and handouts or flipbooks?
4. *Practice:* Did you practice with your visuals?

3. Nonverbal delivery skills: how you look and sound

See Chapter VII

1. *Body language:* Was your body language effective: posture, movement, gestures, facial expression, and eye contact?
2. *Vocal qualities:* Were your vocal qualities effective: inflection, rate, lack of fillers, and enunciation?
3. *Space and objects:* Did you use space and objects around you effectively: seating, height and distance, and objects?
4. *Practice technique:* Did you use a practice technique and make the necessary arrangements?
5. *Relaxation technique:* Did you use a relaxation technique?

CONSULT/IOIN MEETING CHECKLIST

1. Group facilitation skills: what you say

See Chapter V

1. *In advance:* Did you prepare in advance by setting the objective, setting the agenda, and delegating roles?
2. *During the meeting:* Did you facilitate participation during the meeting by opening and closing effectively and encouraging others throughout the meeting?
3. *Decision making and follow up:* Did you make a decision effectively? Did you follow up with a permanent record and an action plan?

2. Group facilitation skills: nonverbal listening skills

See Chapter VII

1. *Attending skills:* Did you use effective attending skills: posture of involvement, eye contact, distance, and elimination of barriers?
2. *Encouraging skills:* Did you use effective encouraging skills: door openers, open-ended questions, attentive silence, and attention?
3. *Following skills:* Did you use effective following skills: paraphrasing content, paraphrasing feelings, and note-taking or recording if appropriate?

APPENDIX A

Formats: for Memos, Reports, and Letters

This appendix provides some example formats for memos, reports, and letters. However, memorizing rigid format rules is not essential because . . .

- Effective strategy and writing skills (Chapters I through IV) will work in any format.
- Most companies provide their own formats. Use the following general guidelines only if your company does not have its own.

In addition, avoid using the formats provided in word-processing programs because most of them do not comply with widely accepted document design issues (explained in Chapter III).

For multiple detailed examples of all three formats, refer to the *Franklin Covey Style,* cited on page 181.

MEMOS

Standard elements of a memo

1. Date
2. "To" heading: reader's name or distribution list
3. "From" heading: your name
4. "Subject" heading: captures attention, describes contents, has "stand-alone sense," as described on page 52
5. Signature: informal, sign your first name next to the "From" heading; semiformal, sign your initials next to the "From" heading; formal, sign with a closing at the end

Sample memo formats

To:
From:
Date:
Subject:

Date:
Subject:
To:
From:

Subject:	Date:
To:	From:

REPORTS

Standard elements of a report

Introductory material

- *Cover letter or memo:* Usually includes reason for writing, authorization for the report, goal, scope and limits, acknowledgments, and audience appeals.
- *Title page:* Title (summary of focus, not vague generalization), name and position of writer(s) and reader(s), and the date.
- *Table of contents:* Outlines major sections of the report. Can include preliminary information (numbered with small roman numerals, i, ii, iii), main and secondary sections (pages numbered with arabic numerals, 1, 2, 3), Appendices (usually lettered Appendix A, Appendix B), exhibits (usually numbered Exhibit I, Exhibit II), and list of illustrations.
- *Executive summary or abstract:* Summarizes the main ideas. Should make sense on its own, because many readers will read only this part. Should summarize your conclusions, recommendations, or implementation steps, not just say, "Five conclusions are reached."

Body of the report

- *Introduction:* Builds reader interest, explains why you're writing, previews your organization. (See pages 62–63 for more information on how to write an introduction.) The introduction is not the same as an executive summary or an abstract.
- *Conclusions, recommendations, findings, and methodology:* Organized clearly with effective headings and subheadings. (See pages 52–54 for more on headings.)

Supplementary information (optional)

- *Appendices:* Supplementary documents such as tables of data, samples of forms, copies of questionnaires, and financial statements. Your reader should not have to read your Appendices to follow your main points in the report.
- *Exhibits:* Supplementary charts and graphs.
- *List of illustrations.*

For a more detailed book specifically on report writing, see the *Guide to Report Writing*, cited on page 181.

LETTERS

Standard elements of a letter

Heading: tells where letter came from and when it was written

- Where: on letterhead paper, at least two lines below letterhead; on plain paper, about an inch from top
- What: on letterhead, date only; on plain paper, three lines: two-line return address, then date

Inside address: tells name and address of person to whom you're writing

- Where: at least two lines below date
- What: *usually five lines:* name, title, company or organization, two-line address; *sometimes four lines:* name and title, company or organization, two-line address

Salutation: addresses reader

- Where: below the inside address. Skip one line before and after the salutation; the salutation is followed by a colon (formal) or comma (informal)
- What: Dear Mr. or Dear Ms. or Dear First Name or Dear Title
  (See page 166 for ideas on how to avoid sexist salutations.)

Subject line (optional): introduces subject

- Where: usually two lines below salutation, centered
- What: phrase to describe subject of letter

Body: discusses subject

- Where: beginning two lines below salutation
- What: as many paragraphs as needed

Closing:

- Where: below the final paragraph. Skip one line before and after the closing.
- What: closing such as

Formal:	Yours truly,
Semiformal:	Sincerely,
Informal:	Cordially,

Signature:

- Where: usually, your signature in ink first, followed by your typed name and title, three to five lines below closing
- What: written signature and typed name and title

Optional: typist, enclosure notification, and copies:

- Where: at least two lines below your typed name and title
- What: (1) can contain your initials in capital letters followed by typist's initials in lowercase; (2) if the letter contains enclosures, enclosure notation goes next; (3) if you are sending copies of the letter to other people, copy notation goes next

  MM:cb

  Enclosure

  cc: Sarah Morgan

Letter formats

Option 1: Full block format

Begin all lines at the left margin.

Company Letterhead

Date

Name
Company
Address
Address

Salutation:

Masthron oltry sirton yotad newbet ekt sretcatahe. Torom hitwed locial koodreoy awit rof resanture of aylow niote criten? Oterbirln omar knille freb doof noidnc. Rewsna 350 gintheoms apn tom forme rekam hos wolloh littlge.

Gnkid tubo ptematt yan norku now lewner oz reay diboter etaryon sellony oiytf nersow. Soger doef retaw ellsw tnemeo stin yo teicor sretem bptse hilpen. Nthron osltry sirton yotad neewbet ehlt sretcat ahc hitwed hip locial koodreoy. Awit rof resanture ao aylow whit nioteco.

Closing,

Signature

Option 2: Modified block format The date, closing, and signature begin to the right of center. Paragraphs start at the left margin.

Company Letterhead

Date

Name
Company
Address
Address

Salutation:

Masthron oltry sirton yotad newbet ekt sretcatahe. Torom hitwed locial koodreoy awit rof resanture of aylow niote criten? Oterbirln omar knille freb doof noidnc. Rewsna 350 gintheoms apn tom forme rekam hos wolloh littlge.

Gnkid tubo ptematt yan norku now lewner oz reay diboter etaryon sellony oiytf nersow. Soger doef retaw ellsw tnemeo stin yo teicor sretem bptse hilpen. Nthron osltry sirton yotad neewbet ehlt sretcat ahc hitwed hip locial koodreoy. Awit rof resanture ao aylow whit nioteco.

Closing,

Signature

Option 3: Semiblock format The date, closing, and signature begin to the right of center. Paragraphs are indented five spaces.

Company Letterhead

Date

Name
Company
Address
Address

Salutation:

Masthron oltry sirton yotad newbet ekt sretcatahe. Torom hitwed locial koodreoy awit rof resanture of aylow niote criten? Oterbirln omar knille freb doof noidnc. Rewsna 350 gintheoms apn tom forme rekam hos wolloh littlge.

Gnkid tubo ptematt yan norku now lewner oz reay diboter etaryon sellony oiytf nersow. Soger doef retaw ellsw tnemeo stin yo teicor sretem bptse hilpen. Nthron osltry sirton yotad neewbet ehlt sretcat ahc hitwed hip locial koodreoy. Awit rof resanture ao aylow whit nioteco.

Closing,

Signature

APPENDIX B

Inclusive Language

Use language that reflects the multicultural reality of business today—language that shows awareness of the global community, that includes rather than excludes, and that is unbiased rather than biased.

Prefer	Avoid
For countries and cultures	
Cultural norms: Most people behave in a certain way most of the time; stated in nonjudgmental, descriptive terms	Stereotypes: All people behave in a certain way all of the time; stated in judgmental, negative terms
Asian	Oriental
United States	America (which could refer to Canada, South America, etc.)
Developing countries	Third World countries
For genders	
Terms that include men and women	Terms that imply that men are the only people in the world
He or she, they or them	He or his (when talking about people in general)
You folks, you people	You guys
Artificial, staff hours	Manmade, man hours
Businessperson, supervisor	Businessman, Foreman
Sales representative	Salesman
Dear Sir or Madam:	Dear Sir:
Dear Investment Manager:	Gentlemen:
Dear Customer:	
No salutation, just a subject line, e.g., "Job Opening at XYZ Corporation"	

APPENDIX C

Grammar and Usage

This appendix contains an alphabetical listing of common errors and problems in grammar and usage.

Agreement between pronoun and antecedent

1. Make sure that your pronoun agrees with its antecedent. Use a singular pronoun to refer to antecedents such as *person, woman, man, kind, each, either, neither, another, anyone, somebody, one, everybody,* and *no one.*

   Each of the committee members agrees to complete **his** assignment before the next meeting.

   (To avoid possible sexist connotations implicit in the masculine singular pronouns, see the previous page.)

2. Use the noun nearer the verb to determine the pronoun for subjects joined by *or* or *nor.*

   Neither Cameron nor Seth has completed **his** (not *their*) memo.

   Either the manager or her subordinates have made **their** (not *her*) group's proposal.

3. Use a singular pronoun for collective nouns.

   The group is preparing **its** (not *their*) statement.

Agreement between subject and verb

1. Make sure that your verb agrees with your subject, which may not be the nearest noun.

   The **risks** of a takeover **seem** great.

   The **risk** of a takeover **seems** great.

2. Use the noun nearer the verb to determine the verb for subjects linked by *or* or *nor, either . . . or,* and *neither . . . nor.*

   Either the Art Department or the Editorial Department **has** the copy.

3. Use a singular verb for collective nouns, such as *group, family, committee.*

   The committee **is** meeting after lunch.

4. Use a singular verb for subjects such as *each, either, another, anyone, someone, something, one, everybody, no one,* and *nothing.*

   Each of us **is** . . .
   Another one of the members **has** . . .
   Either of them **decides** . . .

Comma and dash splices

1. Never put two sentences together separated only by a comma or a dash.

   Incorrect comma splice: The company suffers from financial problems, it has great potential in research and development.

   Incorrect dash splice: The company suffers from financial problems—it has great potential in research and development.

2. Watch out for comma and dash splices especially when you use conjunctive adverbs such as *consequently, hence, however, nevertheless, therefore,* and *thus.*

   Incorrect comma splice: The company suffers from financial problems, however, it has great potential in research and development.

   Incorrect dash splice: The company suffers from financial problems—however, it has great potential in research and development.

3. Separate comma and dash splices with a period, a semicolon, or a subordinator.

   Separated with period: The company suffers from financial problems. However, it has great potential in research and development.

   Separated with semicolon, implying that the two clauses are of equal importance: The company suffers from financial problems; however, it has great potential in research and development.

   Subordinated first clause, implying that the first clause is less important: Although it suffers from financial problems, the company has great potential in research and development.

See also "Run-on sentences," page 172.

Dangling modifiers

See "Modifiers," below.

Dash splices

See "Comma and dash splices," on the previous page.

Fragments

1. Do not carelessly write a sentence fragment as if it were a complete sentence.

   Incorrect fragment, missing a verb: Especially during the October buying season.

   Incorrect fragment, subordinated subject and verb only: When the October buying season arrives.
2. Do use fragments carefully for emphasis, parallelism, and conversational tone.

   Fragments used correctly for emphasis: Out loud. On your feet. With your visual aids.

Modifiers

1. To avoid confusing your reader, place your modifiers as close as possible to the words they modify.
2. Avoid unclear modifiers.

   Unclear: The task force seemed sure **on Thursday** the resolution would pass.

   Clear: **On Thursday,** the task force seemed sure . . .

   Clear: The task force seemed sure the resolution would pass **on Thursday.**
3. Avoid "dangling modifiers"—modifiers misplaced at the beginning of your sentence. The opening phrase (before the comma) must refer to the subject of your independent clause.

   Wrong: Young and inexperienced, **the task** seemed easy to Lindsay. ("The task" is not "young and inexperienced.")

   Right: Young and inexperienced, **Lindsay** thought the task seemed easy.

   Wrong: When calling on a client, **negotiation techniques** are important. ("Negotiation techniques" are not "calling on a client.")

   Right: **Salespeople** calling on a client will find **negotiation techniques** important.

Parallelism

Express ideas of equal importance in grammatical structures of equal importance.

- Parallel adjectives

  Wrong: She was sensitive and a big help.

  Right: She was sensitive and helpful.

- Parallel nouns

  Wrong: The new manager is a genius, a leader, and works hard.

  Right: The new manager is a genius, a leader, and a hard worker.

- Parallel verbs

  Wrong: The workers should arrive on time, correct their own mistakes, and fewer sick days will be used.

  Right: The workers should arrive on time, correct their own mistakes, and use less sick leave.

- Parallel bullet points

  The president announced plans to
  - trim the overseas staff
  - cut the domestic marketing budget
  - better quality control

  The president announced plans to
  - trim the overseas staff
  - cut the domestic marketing budget
  - improve quality control

- Parallel comparisons

  Wrong: First identifying yourself is more effective than to start right off with your sales pitch.

  Right: First identifying yourself is more effective than starting right off with your sales pitch.

- Parallel repeated words

  Wrong: He hands in his payroll sheets, data cards, and his time report on the first of the month.

  Right: He hands in his payroll sheets, his data cards, and his time report on the first of the month *or* He hands in his payroll sheets, data cards, and time report on the first of the month.

Pronoun agreement

See "Agreement between pronoun and antecedent," page 167.

Pronoun case

1. *Use the proper case form* to show the function of pronouns in a sentence.

Case Forms

Subjective	I	he/she	you	we	they	who
Objective	me	him/her	you	us	them	whom
Possessive	my (mine)	his/hers	yours	our (ours)	their (theirs)	whose
Reflexive/ intensive	myself	himself/ herself	yourself	ourselves	themselves	

2. *Use the subjective case* when the pronoun is the subject. Watch out for
   - Compound subjects

     He and **I** finished the job. **We** (not *Us*) managers finished the job.
   - Subject complements

     That may be **she** (not *her*). It was **she who** paid the bill.
3. *Use the objective case* when the pronoun is the sentence object, indirect object, or object of a preposition. Watch out for
   - Sentence objects

     The auditors finally left **him** and **me** (not *he* and *I*).
   - Prepositions

     Just **between you** and **me** (not *you* and *I*) . . .
   - Whom: Use for the object of the sentence, subordinate clause, or preposition.

     Whom did you contact at ABC Company?

     The new chairperson, **whom** we met at the cocktail party, starts work today.

     For **whom** is the message intended?
4. *Use the possessive* to show ownership. Watch out for
   - Gerunds (*-ing* verbs used as nouns)

     We were surprised at **his** (not *him*) resigning.

5. *Use the intensive and reflexive* for emphasis. Watch out for
   - Misuse of *myself:* (Don't use *myself* if you can substitute *I* or *me.*)

     Julia and **I** (not *myself*) designed the market survey.

     He gave the book to Lauren and **me** (not *myself*).

Run-on sentences

1. Never stick two sentences together with a comma, dash, or no punctuation at all.

   Run-on sentence with incorrect comma (comma splice): The company suffers from financial problems, however, it has great potential in research and development.

   Run-on sentence with incorrect dash (dash splice): The company suffers from financial problems—however, it has great potential in research and development.

   Run-on sentence with no punctuation: The company suffers from financial problems however it has great potential in research and development.

2. Separate run-on sentences with a period, a semicolon, or a subordinator.

   Separated with period: The company suffers from financial problems. However, it has great potential in research and development.

   Separated with semicolon, implying that the two clauses are of equal importance: The company suffers from financial problems; however, it has great potential in research and development.

   Subordinated first clause, implying that first clause is less important: Although it suffers from financial problems, the company has great potential in research and development.

Subject–verb agreement

See "Agreement between subject and verb," pages 167–168.

If English is your second language, you may also want to consult *Guide for Internationals: Culture, Communication, and ESL,* cited on page 181.

APPENDIX D

Punctuation

This appendix contains an alphabetical guide to punctuation.

Apostrophe

1. Use an apostrophe to form the possessive of a noun or a pronoun.
   - For nouns (singular or plural) not ending in an *s* or *z* sound, add the apostrophe and *s:*

     Smith's account
     women's rights
     one's own

   - For singular nouns ending in an *s* or *z* sound, add the apostrophe and *s:*

     my boss's office

   - For plural nouns ending in an *s* or *z* sound, add only the apostrophe:

     The Smiths' account
     four dollars' worth

   - For hyphenated compounds, use an apostrophe in the last word only:

     my mother-in-law's idea

   - Differentiate between individual and group possession:

     Garcia and McGrath's account (joint ownership)
     Garcia's and McGrath's accounts (individual ownership)

2. Use an apostrophe to mark the omission of letters in contractions.

they are	they're
fiscal 2006	fiscal '06

3. Use an apostrophe and *s* to form the plural of lowercase letters and of abbreviations followed by periods. When needed to prevent confusion, use the apostrophe and *s* to form the plural of capital letters and abbreviations not followed by periods.

   b's
   M.B.A.'s
   J's or Js
   MBA's or MBAs

4. Do not use an apostrophe with the pronouns *his, its, ours, yours, theirs*, and *whose* or with nonpossessive plural nouns.

   Their department contributed the financial data; ours (not *our's*) added the artwork.

5. Do not confuse *its* with *it's* or *whose* with *who's*.

   Its filing system is antiquated. (its filing system = the filing system of it)

   It's an antiquated filing system. (it's = it is)

   She is an accountant **whose** results are reliable. (whose results = the results of whom)

   She is an accountant **who's** reliable. (who's = who is)

Colon

1. Use a colon as an introducer: to show that what follows will illustrate, explain, or clarify. What follows the colon may be a list, a quotation, a clause, or a word.

   The CEO's decision is final: we will maintain an open-door policy with the press.

   The CEO decided we will do the following: generate a list of potential questions, hold practice interview sessions, and give each person individual feedback after the sessions.

2. Use a colon as a separator between a salutation and the rest of the letter, a title and a subtitle, a chapter and verse of the Bible or Qur'an, and the hour and the minute.

   Dear Ms. Schmidt:

   Guide to Managerial Communication: Effective Business Writing and Speaking

Comma

1. Use a comma to separate independent clauses joined by *and, but, or, nor, for*.

   A long independent clause like this one is perfectly fine, but you need a comma before the coordinator and this second independent clause.

2. Use a comma after introductory transitions and phrases.

   Always use a comma after an introductory transition (such as *however, for example, in the second place*).

   If you find that you have a fairly long introductory phrase at the beginning of your sentence, use a comma before your independent clause (as shown in this sentence).

3. Use a comma to separate items in a parallel series of words, phrases, or subordinate clauses.

   He arranged his pens, pencils, calendar, calculator, and papers on the desk.

4. Use a comma to set off incidental information in the middle of the sentence.

   Incidental information in the middle of the sentence, like this, should be set off with commas.

   Midsentence transitions, moreover, are enclosed in commas.

5. In general, insert a comma whenever you would have a light, natural pause, or whenever necessary to prevent misunderstanding.

Dash

1. Use the dash where you would use a comma when you want a stronger summary or a more emphatic break. Use a dash to emphasize interruptions, informal breaks in thought, or parenthetical remarks—especially if they are strong or contain internal commas.

   Use the dash for a stronger—more emphatic—break.

2. Do not use a dash in place of a period or in place of a semicolon between two independent clauses.

   Do not do this—do not join two complete sentences with a dash.

3. Type a dash—with no space before or after the surrounding words—as two hyphens. Most word processing programs have a keystroke option for creating a real dash.

Exclamation point

Use extremely sparingly to express strong emotions.

Hyphen

1. Use a hyphen between compound adjectives to distinguish between the modifier and the noun.

   high-speed computer
   light-emitting diode

   A hyphen is not necessary if the compound adjectives make up an extremely prevalent term.

   venture capital firm
   virtual reality games

2. Use a hyphen for triple compound adjectives.

   cut-and-paste editing
   ultra-high-density chip

Italics (or underlining)

1. Italics and underlining are used interchangeably for titles. With typewriters, writers use underlining; with computers, writers use italics.
2. Use italics for titles of separate publications (books, magazines, and newspapers) and titles of movies, television series, operas, and other long musical compositions.
3. Use italics for unusual foreign words; words, letters, or numbers referred to as such (for example, There are two *m*'s in *accommodate*); and for emphatic typography (see pages 58–59).

Parentheses

1. Use parentheses for unemphatic parenthetical remarks.

   Unlike dashes—which emphasize the importance of what they surround—parentheses minimize the importance (of what they surround).

2. Use parentheses for defining a new term or new abbreviation.

   The Chicago Board Options Exchange (CBOE) provides more liquidity than traditional over-the-counter options markets.

3. Use parentheses to enclose enumerators within a sentence, such as (1) letters and (2) numbers.

4. Punctuate correctly around parentheses.
   - (If an entire sentence is within the parentheses, like this sentence, place the period inside too.)
   - If just part of the sentence is within the parentheses, as in this sentence, place the period or comma outside the parentheses (like this).

Period

1. Use a period to mark the end of declarative sentences.
2. Use a period to mark most abbreviations.
3. Use three spaced periods, called an ellipsis mark, to indicate the omissions of words in a quoted passage. If the omitted material falls at the end of the sentence, the ellipsis should be preceded by a period.

Question mark

Use only after direct questions, not after indirect questions.

Direct question: "What are you doing?"
Indirect question: He asked what I was doing.

Quotation marks

1. Use quotation marks to enclose all direct quotations from speech or writing. Long prose quotations—more than 10 lines—are usually set off by single spacing and indentation and lack quotation marks unless these appear in the original.
2. Use quotation marks to enclose minor titles (short stories, essays, poems, songs, television shows, and articles from periodicals) and subdivisions of books.
3. Use quotation marks to enclose words used in a special sense or quoted from another context.
4. Do not use quotation marks for common nicknames, bits of humor, or trite or well-known expressions.
5. Punctuate correctly around quotation marks.
   - Always place the period and comma within the quotation marks.
   - Always place the colon and semicolon outside the quotation marks.

- Place the dash, the question mark, and the exclamation point within the quotation marks when they apply only to the quoted matter; place them outside when they apply to the whole sentence.

  He called to say, "Your idea stinks!"
  (punctuation refers to quoted matter only)

  I can't believe he called back to say, "Actually, I like your idea"!
  (punctuation refers to the whole sentence)

6. Use single quotation marks to enclose a quotation or a minor title within a quotation.

   "Use single quotation marks when you have a minor title within a quotation, such as 'Auld Lang Syne,' in this quoted sentence."

Semicolon

1. Use a semicolon to join two closely connected independent clauses of equal importance.

   A semicolon indicates a close connection between two independent clauses of equal importance; these clauses will not be joined in addition by a coordinator *(and, but, or, nor, for).*

2. Use a semicolon to join two independent clauses even if they have a transitional word between them.

   A semicolon indicates a close connection between two independent clauses of equal importance; **however**, don't forget the use of the semicolon to separate independent clauses with a transitional word between them (like *however* in this sentence).

3. Use a semicolon to separate items in a series when your list contains internal commas.

   Use a semicolon to separate items in a series when your list is complex, containing internal commas; when you need stronger punctuation, in order to show where the stronger breaks are; and when you want to avoid confusing your readers, who might get lost with only commas to guide them.

4. Do not use the semicolon to separate items in a list unless the list contains internal commas.

If English is your second language, you may also want to see *Guide for Internationals: Culture, Communication, and ESL*, cited on page 181.

Bibliography

This bibliography is selective, not comprehensive. I included the best references I could find, even if they're not the newest. Some of these articles are "classic"—that is, not recently published but nevertheless crucial—on timeless topics. Others are recent, providing cutting-edge research on more current topics.

Chapter 1: Communication Strategy

Communicator Strategy

French, J. and B. Raven, "The Bases of Social Power," in *Studies in Social Power*, D. Cartwright (ed.). Ann Arbor: University of Michigan Press, 1959.

Kotter, J., *Power and Influence*. New York: The Free Press, 1985.

Tannenbaum, R. and W. Schmidt, "How to Choose a Leadership Pattern," *Harvard Business Review*, March–April 1958, 95–101.

Thompson, M., "The Skills of Inquiry and Advocacy: Why Managers Need Both," *Management Communication Quarterly*, August 1993, 95–106.

Audience Strategy

Cialdini, R., "Harnessing the Science of Persuasion," *Harvard Business Review*, October 2001, 72–79.

Conger, J., "The Necessary Art of Persuasion," *Harvard Business Review*, May 1998, 84–95.

Robbins, S., *Organizational Behavior*, 11th ed. Upper Saddle River, NJ: Prentice Hall, 2004.

Thomas, J., *Guide to Managerial Persuation and Influence*. Upper Saddle River, NJ: Prentice Hall, 2004.

Williams, G. and R. Miller, "Change the Way You Persuade," *Harvard Business Review,* May 2002, 65–73.

Yates, J., "Persuasion: What the Research Tells Us," Cambridge, MA: MIT Sloan Courseware, 2001.

Message Strategy

Buzan, T. and B. Buzan, *The Mind Map Book.* London: BBC, Consumer Publishing, 2001.

Flower, L. and J. Ackerman, *Problem-Solving Strategies for Writing.* Fort Worth, TX: Harcourt Brace College Publishers, 1998.

Minto, B., *The Pyramid Principle: Present Your Thinking So Clearly That the Ideas Jump Off the Page and into the Reader's Mind,* 3rd ed. London: Minto International, Inc., 2001.

Channel Choice Strategy

DeTienne, K., *Guide to Electronic Communication.* Upper Saddle River, NJ: Prentice Hall, 2002.

Nemiro, J., *Creativity in Virtual Teams.* New York: John Wiley & Sons, 2004.

Culture Strategy

Culturgrams. Provo, UT: Kennedy Center Publications, Brigham Young University, published yearly.

Munter, M., "Cross-Cultural Communication for Managers," *Business Horizons,* May–June 1993, 69–79.

Reynolds, S. and D. Valentine, *Guide to Cross-Cultural Communication.* Upper Saddle River, NJ: Prentice Hall, 2004.

Tannen, D., *Talking From 9 to 5: Women and Men at Work.* New York: Quill, 2001.

Chapters II, III, IV: Writing

Alred, G. *et al.*, *The Business Writer's Handbook*, 7th ed. New York: St. Martins Press, 2003.

Bringhurst, R., *The Elements of Typographical Style*. London: Frances Lincoln Ltd, 2004.

Fielden, J., "What Do You Mean You Don't Like My Style?" *Harvard Business Review*, May–June 1982, 128–139.

—— and R. Dulek, "How to Use Bottom-Line Writing in Corporate Communications," *Business Horizons*, July–August 1984, 24–30.

Flower, L. and J. Ackerman, *Problem-Solving Strategies for Writing*. Fort Worth, TX: Harcourt Brace College Publishers, 1998.

Franklin Covey Style Guide For Business and Technical Communication, 3rd ed. Salt Lake City, UT: Franklin Covey Co., 1999.

Munter, M., J. Rymer, and P. Rogers, "Business Email: Guidelines for Users," *Business Communications Quarterly*, March 2003.

Murray, D., *Write to Learn*, 8th ed. Independence, KY: Heinle, 2004.

Netzley, M. and C. Snow, *Guide to Report Writing*. Upper Saddle River, NJ: Prentice Hall, 2002.

Reynolds, S. and D. Valentine, *Guide for Internationals: Culture, Communication, and ESL*. Upper Saddle River, NJ: Prentice Hall, 2006.

Williams, J., *Style: Ten Lessons in Clarity and Grace*, 8th ed. New York: Longman, 2004.

Chapters V, VI, and VII: Presentations

Argenti, P., *Corporate Communication*, 3rd ed. Boston: Irwin/McGraw-Hill, 2003 (Chapter 6 on media relations).

Baney, J., *Guide to Interpersonal Communication*. Upper Saddle River, NJ: Prentice Hall, 2004.

Bolton, R., *People Skills: How to Assert Yourself, Listen to Others, and Resolve Conflicts*. New York: Simon & Schuster, 1987.

Cooper, M., *Change Your Voice, Change Your Life*. Manhattan Beach, CA: Wilshire Press, 1996.

Howell, J., *Tools for Facilitating Team Meetings.* Seattle, WA: Integrity Publishing, 1995.

Jay, A. and R. Jay, *Effective Presentation*, 2nd ed. London: Financial Times Management, 2004.

Knapp, M., *Nonverbal Communication in Human Interaction*, 6th ed. Wadsworth Publishing Company, 2005.

Munter, M. and M. Netzley, *Guide to Meetings.* Upper Saddle River, NJ: Prentice Hall, 2002.

——— and D. Paradi, *Guide to PowerPoint.* Upper Saddle River, NJ: Prentice Hall, 2007.

——— and L. Russell, *Guide to Presentations.* Upper Saddle River, NJ: Prentice Hall, 2002.

———, "How to Conduct a Successful Media Interview," *California Management Review,* Summer 1983, 143–150.

Schenkler, I. and T. Herrling, *Guide to Media Relations.* Upper Saddle River, NJ: Prentice Hall, 2004.

Tufte, E., *The Cognitive Style of PowerPoint.* Cheshire, CT: Graphics Press, 2003.

———, *The Visual Display of Quantitative Information.* Cheshire, CT: Graphics Press, 2001.

Walker, C., *Learn to Relax.* Carlsbad, CA: Penton Overseas, 2003, CD-ROM.

White, J., *Color for Impact: How Color Can Get Your Message Across—or Get in the Way.* Berkeley, CA: Strathmoor Press, 1997.

Williams, R., *The Non-Designer's Design Book: Design & Typographic Principles for the Visual Novice*, 2nd ed. Berkeley, CA: Peachpit Press, 2003.

Zelazny, G., *Say It with Charts: The Executive's Guide to Visual Communication*, 4th ed. New York: McGraw-Hill, 2001.

———, *Say It with Presentations.* Burlington, MA: Adobe Systems, e-book.

Index

A

Abstracts, in reports, 160
Accent color (in visual aids): choosing, 115; tying message title to, 120; overriding default colors for, 129
Action plan (ending with): in writing, 63; in presentations, 91; in meetings, 101
Agenda: as preview in presentation, 89; preparing, for meeting, 98; visual aids for, 110; repeated use of, 112; message title in, 119; concept diagram for, 124
Agreement: pronoun/antecedent, 167; subject/verb, 167–168
Animation (in visual aids): how to use, 117, 133; to avoid overload, 128; as advantage of computer projection, 131
Antecedent, agreement of, 167
Apostrophe, 173–174
Appendices, in report, 160
Arrows (in visual aids): tied to message title, 120; in concept diagrams, 124–125
Attending skills, 153
Audience: strategy for:
- analysis of, 10–14
- persuasion of, 15–17
- message strategy for, 18–22
- channel choice for, 23
- cultural effects on, 30

writing techniques for:
- document design, 52–59
- signposts to show connection, 59–63
- brevity, 70–75
- style, 76–83

speaking techniques for:
- structure, 88–91
- questions and answers, 93–96
- meetings, 97–101
- visual aids, 130
- connecting with, 149

Audience benefits, 15
Audience Memory Curve: defined, 19; implications of, 19–22; for structuring a presentation, 88
Audioconferences, 26, 104

B

Back-and-forth references (in writing), 61
Backward look/forward look transitions (in speaking), 90
Backup slides, 110, 111, 112
Balance theory, 17
Bar chart, 120, 121, 122
Blast email, 24
Blast fax, 24
Boards and flipcharts, 131, 134, 137. See also Visual aids

Body language: in videoconferences, 105; for presentations, 140–141; relaxation techniques for, 146–151; for listening, 157. See also Nonverbal Communication
Boldface. See Typography
Bolton, R., 152
Brainstorming: as a prewriting technique, 37; meeting skills for, 97–101; visual aids for, 137
Breathing, vocal exercises for, 146, 147, 150
Brevity, techniques for, in writing, 70–75
Broadcasting, 26
"Build" function (in visuals). See Animation
Bullet points: parallelism in, 54, 170; to break up overly long sentences, 75; building, 117; not misusing, indentation for, 127
Buzan, T., 38

C

Camera, use of: in videoconferencing, 104–105; in media presentations, 106
Capital letters: limiting use of, in writing, 59; avoiding in visual aids, 116
Cards, use of, in speaking, 92
Carnegie, D., 148
Case: in visuals, 116; in grammar, 171
Channels of communication: audience expectations for, 12; choosing strategically, 23–28; cultural differences in, 30–31; choosing before writing, 36
Chartjunk, avoiding, 129
Charts: choosing, 131, 135; using, 137. See also Visual Aids
Checklist: for communication strategy, 32; for macro-writing, 84; for micro-writing, 85; for tell/sell presentations, 156; for consult/join meetings, 157
Chevrons (in concept diagrams), 125
Clip Art (limiting use of), 129
Closings: audience strategy for, 17; message strategy for, 18–21; in writing, 63; in tell/sell presentations, 91; summary slide for, 111; for meetings, 100–101; practicing, for presentations, 144; in letters, 161
Coherence. See Signposts
Colon, 174
Color, use of, in visual aids, 114–115; tying to message title, 120; avoiding chartjunk with, 129
Column chart, 120, 121, 123
Comma, 175
Comma splice, 168
Common ground: for credibility, 9; for audience motivation, 16
Communication objective: defined, 4; examples of, 5
Communication strategy. See Strategy
Communication style. See Style
Composition process, for writing, 36–43
Computers: as channel choice, 23–27; for writing composition, 41–42; as visual aids, 130, 131
Concept diagrams, 124–125
Conceptual parallelism, 54
Conclusions. See Closings
Conference calls, 26, 104

Conflict, controlling: during questions and answers, 96; during meetings, 100
Consensus, achieving, in meetings, 101
Consistency principle, 17
Consult/join style: when to use, 6–7; channel choice for, 25; structure for, 97–101; visual aids for, 137; nonverbal skills for, 152–155
Contractions, use of, in writing style, 77; use of apostrophe for, 173
Conversation (face-to-face), 28, 152–155
Credibility: analysis of, 8–9; motivating through, 16; effect on message strategy, 20–21; cultural differences in, 30; in introduction for writing, 63; in opening for presentation, 89
Culture, effect on: strategy, 21, 29–31; questions and answers, 93; use of color, 115; nonverbal behavior, 139; listening, 153; inclusive language, 166

D

Dangling (misplaced) modifier, 169
Dash, 175
Dash splice, 168
Decision making, in meetings, 100–101
Decks (for presentations): using message titles in, 119; choosing to use, 131; cueing audience with, 133
Delivery: body language for, 140–141; vocal qualities for, 142; space and objects for, 143; practice and arrangements for, 144–145; relaxation for, 146–151
Diagrams, 124–125. See also Visual aids
"Dim" function (in visuals). See Animation
Direct approach, in message strategy: when to use, 19–20; examples of, 22; effect of culture on, 30
Distance: cross-cultural implications for, 31; in presentation arrangements, 143; for listening skills, 153
Document design techniques: for entire document, 52–58; for paragraphs, 66
"Door-in-the-face" technique, 17
Drafting process: in writing, 41; in group writing, 48–49
Dress: for television, 106; for presentations, 143

E

Editing: process for, 42; inverted pyramid for, 43; in group writing, 49; for macro-writing, 52–67; for micro-writing, 70–83; of speech manuscript, 103; of visual aids, 128–129; for correctness, 167–178
Electronic mail (email): as channel choice, 24; use of, for meetings, 27; techniques for using, 46–47
Electronic meetings (EMS), as channel choice, 27
Ellipsis, 177
Ellis, A., 148
Email: as channel choice, 24; use of, for meetings, 27; techniques for using, 46–47
Emoticons: defined, 24; using, 47
Emotional level, of audience, 13–14

Empathy: for audience analysis, 11; for listening, 152–155. See also Audience
Emphasis: in messages, 19–20; in typography, 58–59; using accent color for, 115, 120
Endings. See Closings
Enunciation, 142
Equipment: using, for media presentations, 106; choosing, for visual aids, 130–131; practicing with, 132–135
Ewing, D., 83
Exclamation point, 176
Executive summary, as standard element of report, 160
Exercise, to combat stage fright, 146–147, 150
Exhibits, as standard element of report, 160. See also Visual aids
Expertise, in credibility, 8–9
Eye contact: cross-cultural differences in, 31; in question-and-answer sessions, 95; with scribe, 99; with equipment, 103; in videoconferences, 105; on television, 106; with visual aids, 135; with decks, 136; with flipcharts, 137; delivery skills for, 141; listening skills for, 153

F

Facial expression, 141, 147
Facilitator, use of, in meetings, 98
Facsimile (fax), as channel choice, 24
Feedback mechanism, 63
Fielden, J., 78
Filler words, 142
Flipbooks. See Decks
Flipcharts: choosing, 131, 135; using, 137. See also Visual aids
Flow chart, 125
Flower, L., 40
Focusing, as technique for efficient composition, 40
Font, use of: in writing, 58–59; in visual aids, 116, 128–129
"Foot-in-the-door" technique, 17
Formality: in channel choice, 23; in writing, 76–81; in speaking, 130, 143
Format: memo, 159; report, 160; letter, 163–165
Fragments, 169
French, J. and B. Raven, 8
"Fruit salad effect," avoiding, 115, 129

G

G and H charts, 125
Gatekeepers, 11
Gathering information, 37
Gender: tendencies by, 30; avoiding bias against, 166
Gerunds, 171
Gestures, in presentations, 141
Goodwill: in credibility, 9; and reciprocity technique, 16
"Grabbers," 88–89. See also Openings
Grammar: agreement between pronoun and antecedent, 167; agreement between subject and verb, 167–168; comma and dash splices, 168; dangling modifiers, 169; fragments, 169; modifiers, 169; parallelism, 170; pronoun case, 171; run-on sentences, 172
Graphs, 121–123. See also Visual aids
Greetings/hospitality, cultural differences in, 31
Ground rules, in meetings, 99
Group writing, 48–49

Guide to: Cross Cultural Communication, 31, 180; Internationals (ESL), 178, 181; Interpersonal Communication, 152, 181; Media Communication, 106, 182; Meetings, 97, 155, 182; PowerPoint, 117, 182; Presentations, 155, 182

H

Hall, E., 113, 153
Hand and arm gestures, 141, 147
Handouts: choosing to use, 131, 133, 135; using, 141
Headings and subheadings: writing first, to overcome writer's block, 44; in email, 47; in writing, 52–59; on visuals, 118–120; on flipcharts, 137; in reports, 160; in letters, 161
Height, above audience, 143
"High skim value" (HSV): in email, 47; defined, 52; techniques for, 52–59
Humming, as vocal exercise, 147
Humor: in email, 47; in presentations, 89
Hyphen, 176

I

Idea charts: for organizing writing, 38; examples of, 39; for overcoming writer's block, 44
Image, in credibility, 9
Imperative verbs, 81
Impersonal openings, avoiding overuse of, 71
Impromptu speaking, 103
Indentations: in lists, 56; to show organization, 57; in visual aids, 127
Indirect approach, in message strategy: when to use, 21; examples of, 22; effect of culture on, 30
Inflection, 142
Internal enumeration (in sentences), 74
Interviewing: as method to gather information, 37; impromptu speaking for, 103; with the media, 106; listening techniques for, 152–155
Introductions: writing last, 41, 44; effective, in writing, 62–63; in reports, 160. See also Openings (for speaking)
Isometric exercises, 150
Italics: avoiding, for extended text, 59; using, as punctuation, 176

J

Jacobson, E., 146
Jargon, 82–83
Jay, A., 107
Jokes: in email, 47; in presentations, 89
Justified margins, avoiding, 57

K

Kotter, J., 8

L

Labels for graphs, 123
Last-minute relaxation, 150–151
Legends (avoiding use of), 123, 129
Length: audience expectations regarding, 12; of paragraphs in email, 47; of paragraphs, 55; of sentences, 74–75
Letters: elements of, 161–162; formats for, 163–165
Line breaks (in word charts), 128
Line graph, 121, 122
Linking verbs, avoiding overuse of, 71

Listening: in meetings, 100; techniques for, 152–155
Lists, use of, in writing, 56

M

Macrowriting: editing for, 42–43; defined, 51; document design in, 52–59; signposts to show connections in, 60–63; paragraphs or sections in, 64–67; checklist for, 84
Manuscript speaking, 102–103
Margins (choosing unjustified), 57
Matrix diagrams, 125
Media, dealing with, 106
Medium of communication. See Channels of communication
Meetings: channel choice for, 25–27; structure for, 97–101; using flipcharts for, 137; nonverbal skills for, 152–155
Memos, elements of and formats for, 159
Message structure: persuading through, 17; strategy for, 18–22; cultural aspects of, 30
Message titles (in visual aids): tied to accent color, 115; how to use, 118–120
Microphones, in videoconferences, 105
Microwriting: editing for, 42–43; defined, 69; brevity in, 70–75; style in, 76–83; checklist for, 85
Mind-map, 38
Minimal encouragers (for listening), 100, 154
Minto, B., 38
Modifiers, misplaced, 169
Motivation. See Persuasion
Movement, in speaking, 144
Multi-level documents: headings for, 53; introductions for, 62
Multimedia projection systems, 130–131
Murray, D., 37

N

Nonverbal communication: in channel choice strategy, 24–28; in culture strategy, 31; in videoconferences, 105; in media presentations, 106; importance of, 139; delivery skills for, 140–151; listening skills for, 152–155
Notecards, for speaking, 92
Note-taking: to gather information, 37; on visual aids, 130–131; 136–137; as a listening skill, 155
"Nutshelling" ideas, 40

O

Objectives: benefits of and how to set, 4; examples of, 5; cultural affect on, 29; tying questions back to, 95; setting, before meetings, 98
One-level documents: headings for, 53; introductions for, 62
Open-ended questions: 100, 154
Openings: strategy for:
- persuasion, 17
- message strategy, 18–22

in writing:
- composing last, 41
- introductions, 62–63
- in reports, 160

in speaking:
- in presentations, 88–89, 110, 144
- in meetings, 99

Organization: for audience strategy, 17; for message strategy, 22; process for, in writing, 38–39;

for group writing, 48; document design to show, 52–59; signposts to show, 60–63; for tell/sell presentations, 88–91; for consult/join meetings, 97–101
Outlines: to organize thoughts, 38; as preview for presentations, 89; speaking from, 92. See also Organization
Overhead projectors: choosing, 131; revealing lines in, 134; practicing with, 137. See also Visual aids

P

Paired bar chart, 122
Paragraphs: length of, in email, 47; length of, in traditional writing, 55; use of white space in, 57; effective use of, 64–67
Parallelism: in headings and subheadings, 54; for grammatical correctness, 170
Paraphrasing: during questions and answers, 94; during meetings, 100; for listening, 155
Parentheses, 176–177
Passive voice, 78–81
Period, 168, 172, 177
Persuasion:
- through audience benefits, 15
- through credibility, 16
- through message structure, 17
- cultural differences in, 30
- in document opening and closing, 62–63
- in presentation opening, 88–89
- in closing, 91
See also Audience
Physical relaxation techniques, 146–151
Pie chart, 120, 122, 123
Pitch, 142
Pointer (avoiding use of), 134
Pointing: on visuals, 134; as nonverbal delivery skill, 141
Point size: for documents, 58; for visual aids, 116
Poise, 140
Posture: for presentations, 140; for listening, 153
PowerPoint: template (SlideMaster) for, 110–117; individual slides for, 118–129; equipment for, 130–131; practice with, 132–136; book on, 182
Practice (for speaking): to anticipate questions, 94; for videoconferences, 104; for media presentations, 106; for team presentations, 107; with visual aids, 132–137; for presentations, 144
Prepositions, avoiding overuse of, 72–73
Presentations: channel choice for, 25; structure for, 87–91; team, 107; visual aids for, 109–137; nonverbal delivery skills for, 139–152
Previews: in writing, 61; in speaking, 89; on visual aids, 110
Prewriting, 36–40
Progressive relaxation, 146
Projections/projectors, 130–131. See also Visual aids
Pronouns: use of, in writing style, 77; avoiding sexist, 166; agreement with antecedent, 167; proper case of, 171
Proofreading: for writing, 42; for group writing, 49; for visuals, 129

Punctuation: apostrophe, 173–174; colon, 174; comma, 175; dash, 175; exclamation point, 176; italics, 176; parentheses, 176–177; period, 177; question marks, 177; quotation marks, 177–178; semicolon, 178
Punishment, as persuasion technique, 16
Pyramid: for organizing thoughts, 38–39; inverted, for editing, 43

Q

Question mark, 177
Questions and answers: for presentations, 93–96; for team presentations, 107
Quotation marks, 177

R

Ragged right margins, 57
Rahmun, L., 97
Rank credibility: defined, 9; punishment technique, 16
Rate, in speaking, 142
Recording of ideas, 99, 137, 155
Rehearsal. See Practice
Relaxation to combat stage fright, 146–151
Reports, elements of, 160
Response: as definition of effective communication, 3; ability to receive, in different channels, 23–28
Rhythm: in sentences, 75; in manuscript speaking, 102
"Rivers" of white space, 57
Rogers, P., 46
Room arrangements, 145
Rosen, C., 126
Run-on sentence, 172
Russell, L., 126, 141
Rymer, J., 46

S

Salutations: in letters, 161; avoiding sexist, 166
Sans serif fonts (when to use): in writing, 59; in visual aids, 116
Sarnoff, D., 146
Scatter chart, 122
Scribe, use of, for recording ideas, 99, 137
Seating, 145
Section previews, in writing, 61
Sell style. See Tell/sell style
Semicolon, 178
Sentence case: in writing, 59; in visual aids, 116
Sentences: effective, because of:
- brevity, 70–75
- avoiding overlong, 74–75
- variety and rhythm, 75
- grammatical correctness of, 167–172
Serif fonts: in writing, 59; in visual aids, 116
Sexism, avoiding, in language, 116
Shared values credibility: defined, 9; and "common ground" technique, 16
Signature: in memos, 159; in letters, 162
Signposts, for connection in writing, 60–63, 66–67
"Six by six rule," 126
"Skim value": defined, 51; techniques for, 52–58

SlideMaster, 114–117. See also PowerPoint
Slide projectors, 133, 134. See also Visual aids
Slides. See Visual aids
Space. See Distance
Speaking: structure for, 88–92; visual aids for, 109–137; nonverbal skills for, 138–151
Spot color. See Accent color
Stage fright, how to avoid, 146–151
"Stand-alone sense," in macro-writing, 52–53; in visual aids, 110, 126
Strategy (for communication):
  five components introduced, 3
    - 1: communicator strategy, 4–9
    - 2: audience strategy, 10–17
    - 3: message strategy, 18–22
    - 4: channel choice strategy, 23–28
    - 5: culture strategy, 29–31
  checklist for, 32
  setting before writing, 36
  editing for, 42
  in group writing, 48
  setting before meetings, 98
Structure: for persuasion, 17; for message strategy, 18–22; signposts to show, 60–63, 66; for tell/sell presentations, 88–92; translating into slides, 110–113. See also Organization
Style (communication, model for): introduced, 6–7; audience preferences for, 12; cultural differences in, 29
  in presentation structure:
    - tell/sell presentations, 88–91
    - consult/join meetings, 97–101
  in visual aids:
    - tell/sell visuals, 109–136
    - consult/join visuals, 137
Style (for writing), 76–83
Subheadings. See Headings and subheadings
Subject: heading in email, 46; heading in memo, 159; agreement with verb, 167–168
Summaries: in writing, 63; in speaking, 91; slide for, 111, 119; executive, 160. See also Closings

T

T-charts, 125
Table of contents: in document opening, 62–63; in presentation preview, 89; in report, 160
Tannenbaum, R. and H. Schmidt, model defined, 6
Team presentations, 107
Technology: effect on channel choice, 23–28; effect on visual aids, 130–131
Telecommunications, as channel choice, 26–28
"Telegram language," 126
Telephone, as channel choice, 26, 28
Television, as channel choice, 26
Tell/sell style: when to use, 6–7; channel choice for, 25; structure for, in presentations, 88–91; visual aids for, 109–136; nonverbal delivery skills for, 140–151
Template (for visual aids), 114–117
Thinking: versus strategic message, 18; before writing, 36–40; on your feet, 93–96, 103. See also Organization

Time (saving for audience): by using direct approach, 20; by channel choice, 23–28; by using "high skim value," 52–59; by avoiding wordiness, 70–73; by avoiding passive voice, 79; during questions and answers, 94–96; during meetings, 97–101
Time-management: for strategy:
- by setting objectives, 4
- by choosing channel, 23
for writing:
- by planning, 36–40
- during drafting, 41
- during editing, 42
- by avoiding writer's block, 44–45
- for group writing, 48–49
for speaking:
- during questions and answers, 93–96
- during meetings, 97–101
- during practice sessions, 144
Timekeeper, during meetings, 98
Title case (avoiding): in writing, 59; in visuals, 116
Topic sentences, 64–65, 67
Topic titles (avoiding): in writing, 52; on visuals, 118–119
Trackers (in visual aids), 113
Transitions: defined, 66; examples of, 67; to break up overlong sentences, 74; for speaking, 90; for closings, 91; in team presentations, 107; between visual aids, 133; using commas with, 178. See also Signposts
Tufte, E., 114, 124, 129
Typography, use of: in writing, 58–59; in visual aids, 116–117

U
Underlining: as a document design technique, 59; use of, as punctuation, 176
Unserifed fonts (when to use): in writing, 59; in visuals, 116
Usage, 167–172

V
Venn charts, 125
Verbs: linking, 71; elongated, 73; active or passive, 78–81; agreement of, with subject, 167–168
Video: as communication channel, 26; in videoconferencing, 104–105; in media communications, 106; to analyze delivery, 144; for mental relaxation, 148
Videoconferences: as channel choice, 26; techniques for, 104–105
Visual aids: importance of, 109;
designing:
- for team presentations, 107
- for the presentation as a whole, 110–120
- for each individual slide, 118–129
equipment for: 130–131
practicing with: 107, 132–137, 144
arrangements for: 145
Visualization, to combat stage fright, 148, 149
Vocal relaxation, 147
Voice: active or passive, 78–81; use of, in videoconferences, 105; use of, in presentations, 142; relaxation of, 147; awareness of others' tone of, 155
Voicemail, as channel choice, 28
Volume: in presentations, 142; awareness of others', 155

W

Webcasting, as channel choice, 26
Web page, as channel choice, 25
"What next" steps: in writing, 63; in presentations, 91; in meetings, 101
White boards, 131
White, J., 115
White space: defined, 55; use of, 55–57
Who/whom, 171
Word charts, as visual aids, 126–128
Wordiness (avoiding): in writing, 70–73, 79; in visual aids, 126–128
Words (editing for): wordiness, 70–73; style, 76–83; inclusive use of, 166; grammatical use of, 173–178
Writer's block (avoiding), 44–45
Writing: channel choice for, 24–25; process for composing efficiently, 36–43; in groups, 48–49; macrowriting, 51–67; microwriting, 69–83; formats for, 158–165; grammar for, 167–172; punctuation for, 173–178
Writing style, 76–83

Y

Yates, J., 15
Yoga sigh breath, 146

Z

Zelazny, G., 118, 122